A PLACE CALLED
HEAVEN
DEVOTIONAL

A PLACE CALLED

HEAVEN

DEVOTIONAL

100 Days of Living in the Hope of Eternity

DR. ROBERT
JEFFRESS

BakerBooks

a division of Baker Publishing Group
Grand Rapids, Michigan

© 2021 by Robert Jeffress

Published by Baker Books
a division of Baker Publishing Group
PO Box 6287, Grand Rapids, MI 49516-6287
www.bakerbooks.com

Printed in the United States of America

Library of Congress Cataloging-in-Publication Data
Names: Jeffress, Robert, 1955– author.
Title: A place called heaven devotional : 100 days of living in the hope of
   eternity / Dr. Robert Jeffress.
Description: Grand Rapids, Michigan : Baker Books, a division of Baker
   Publishing Group, 2021.
Identifiers: LCCN 2020018559 | ISBN 9781540900913 (cloth)
Subjects: LCSH: Heaven—Christianity—Prayers and devotions.
Classification: LCC BT846.3 .J445 2021 | DDC 236/.24—dc23
LC record available at https://lccn.loc.gov/2020018559

Some content in this book has been adapted from Robert Jeffress, *A Place Called Heaven: 10 Surprising Truths about Your Eternal Home* (Grand Rapids: Baker Books, 2017).

Published in association with Yates & Yates, www.yates2.com.

21 22 23 24 25 26 27   7 6 5 4 3 2 1

What Difference Does a Future Heaven Make in My Life Today?

> In My Father's house are many dwelling places; if it were not so, I would have told you; for I go to prepare a place for you.
>
> —John 14:2

A few years ago, I went on a one-week trip to London. The city was somewhat unfamiliar to me, and I needed to make certain preparations. I had to stop the newspaper and mail delivery at my house, make sure my cell phone would work in the country I was going to, and change some of my currency from dollars into pounds. Most of all, I needed to make sure I had a valid passport so that when I arrived, I would be allowed to enter that country.

Now, my trip to another country was brief. But did you know the Bible says that every one of us will one day make a trip to a distant country? It will be a one-way trip to a place that is mostly unfamiliar to us. And this destination is not merely a one-week vacation; it will be an eternal destination for every one of us. For those of us who are Christians, that trip will be to a place called heaven.

Jesus assured us that heaven is a real place.

Contrary to what some people believe, heaven is not just some fanciful myth to help dull the pain of the reality of this world. Jesus assured us that heaven is a real place.

Jesus said to His disciples, "In My Father's house are many dwelling places; if it were not so, I would have told you; for I go to prepare a place for you. If I go and prepare a place for you, I will come again and receive you to Myself, that where I am, there you may be also" (John 14:2–3). Jesus is in heaven right now, and He is overseeing the largest construction project in history. He is building our future home in this place He calls heaven.

––––––––––

How does it make you feel to know that Jesus is preparing a place for you in heaven?

What preparations can you begin making today to be ready for your heavenly home?

Lord Jesus, thank You for preparing a place for me in Your Father's house. Help me make the necessary preparations in my life today so I will be ready to enter my heavenly home with You.

Homesick for Heaven

> For indeed in this house we groan, longing to be
> clothed with our dwelling from heaven.
>
> —2 Corinthians 5:2

Very few Christians spend time consciously thinking about heaven. Perhaps you don't spend a lot of time reflecting on your eternal destination either.

Although many Christians are missing out on the hope that comes from reflecting on our heavenly home, I'm pretty sure I understand why. The overwhelming responsibilities of this life often eclipse our thinking about the next life. Not only that, but heaven seems remote. It seems irrelevant to those of us who are busy trying to rear a family, keep a job, or make a living here on earth. Why should we be concerned about heaven?

We all long for that home—that place called heaven.

Though we do not think about heaven often, there are times in life when we long for a better place than earth. Sometimes we experience a disappointment—betrayal by a close friend, an illness, the loss of a loved one, the breakup of an important relationship—that makes us long for something better.

In his book *Disappointment with God*, Philip Yancey observed,

> The Bible never belittles human disappointment . . . but it does add one key word: temporary. What we feel now, we will not

always feel. Our disappointment is itself a sign, an aching, a hunger for something better. And faith is, in the end, a kind of homesickness—for a home we have never visited but have never once stopped longing for.[1]

We all long for that home—that place called heaven.

Have you ever felt homesick for heaven?

How does the hope of heaven change your perspective on the disappointments of this life?

Lord, sometimes I feel overwhelmed by the disappointments of this life. Give me Your perspective on my problems to remember that they are only temporary—until I go home to heaven.

Our Inevitable Journey to a New Destination

Man does not know his time.
—Ecclesiastes 9:12

Why should we study what the Bible teaches about heaven? One reason is that our journey to heaven is both certain and relatively soon.

The Bible talks about the inevitability of our journey to this new destination called heaven. I have also heard one wag quip, "The statistics on death are very impressive: one out of every one dies."

Have you come to grips with the fact that you are going to die? The writer of Ecclesiastes, Solomon, said it this way: "Man does not know his time: like fish caught in a treacherous net and birds trapped in a snare, so the sons of men are ensnared at an evil time when it suddenly falls on them" (9:12).

Our departure from this life is certain, and it is soon.

Death comes suddenly, without any warning. In Genesis 27:2, the patriarch Isaac said, "Behold now, I am old and I do not know the day of my death." And neither do you. Neither do I. Soldiers on a battlefield and patients whose diseases have been labeled "terminal" may understand the reality and certainty of death more clearly than the rest of us, but the truth is, death is just as real and certain for you and me.

The fact that life on earth is very brief should motivate us to use our time wisely. In Psalm 90:12, Moses prayed, "Teach us to number our days and recognize how few they are; help us to spend them as we should" (TLB). Our departure from this life is certain, and it is soon.

———

Have you ever thought of your life as "terminal"?
In what ways does the certainty of your death affect how you are living right now?

Heavenly Father, teach me to number my days and realize that, in light of eternity, my time on earth is short. Help me spend every day You give me in this life in a way that honors You.

Learning to Number Our Days

Teach us to number our days and recognize how
few they are.

—Psalm 90:12 TLB

In Psalm 90:12, Moses prayed, "Teach us to number our days
and recognize how few they are; help us to spend them as we
should" (TLB).

Several years ago, I had a friend who lived by this verse.
He was in his midsixties when I got to know him. I remember
going into his office one day and seeing his blackboard filled
with chalk marks. I asked him, "What are those?" He said,
"The Bible says I will probably live to be age seventy, so those
marks represent how many days I have left before God calls
me home. Every day when I walk into my office, I erase one
mark." The day after his seventieth birthday, he made a new
mark on the chalkboard, and he started
doing that every day to remind himself
he was living on borrowed time. When
we realize the brevity of our lives, we
should live wisely.

*When we realize the
brevity of our lives,
we should live wisely.*

Recognizing how brief our time is on
earth also ought to motivate us to think about heaven.

You may be familiar with the story of Joni Eareckson Tada.
When Joni was a teenager, in 1967, a diving accident caused
her to become a quadriplegic. Since then, Joni has spent a
lot of time thinking about heaven. In her book *Heaven: Your*

Real Home, she wrote, "Heaven may be as near as next year, or next week; so it makes good sense to spend some time here on earth thinking candid thoughts about that marvelous future reserved for us."[1]

Why should we spend time thinking about heaven? Because the choices we make in this life drastically impact the next life God has prepared for us.

If seventy years is the average life span, how many "chalk marks" are left in your life?

Are you living on borrowed time?

How does this perspective affect the way you will live today?

Lord, the future You have reserved for me is beyond what I can imagine. Help me make choices today that will positively impact the eternal life You have prepared for me in heaven.

Perspectives from the Past

For to me, to live is Christ and to die is gain.
—Philippians 1:21

Throughout history, great Christian writers, thinkers, and philosophers have written about heaven. C. S. Lewis wrote,

> If you read history you will find that the Christians who did most for the present world were just those who thought most of the next. . . . It is since Christians have largely ceased to think of the other world that they have become so ineffective in this. Aim at Heaven and you will get earth "thrown in"; aim at earth and you will get neither.[1]

The more we think about the next life, the more effective we become for God in this life.

I have experienced this personally. Three times, I have been serving in a church when God called me to serve in another church. Each time that happened, there was a period after the new church called me during which I had to go back to my old church and finish my work there. Ironically, that was usually my most productive time in that church. I was highly motivated to finish my work because I wanted things to be in good shape when I left. Not only that, I had a certain freedom. I could make the decisions I felt were best without worrying about what other

The more we think about the next life, the more effective we become for God in this life.

14

people thought because, after all, what could they do to me? I was already going someplace else.

That is a good metaphor for what our lives ought to be like here on earth. The fact is, we are all leaving here. Our departure is certain. It will not be long until we go to that place called heaven.

———————

How often do you think about heaven?

What can you do today to allow the certainty of the next life to influence your effectiveness for God in this life?

God, I eagerly anticipate the day when I will be with You in heaven for eternity! In the meantime, help me be diligent and productive in the tasks You have entrusted to me on earth.

Motivation for Effective Living

> All these died in faith, without receiving the promises, but having seen them and having welcomed them from a distance, and having confessed that they were strangers and exiles on the earth.
>
> —Hebrews 11:13

Knowing that our future is secure in heaven ought to motivate us to live effectively for God on earth. That was certainly true of the Old Testament saints such as Abel, Enoch, Noah, Abraham, Isaac, Jacob, and Sarah. Notice what Hebrews 11:13 says about these men and women of faith: "All these died in faith, without receiving the promises, but having seen them and having welcomed them from a distance, and having confessed that they were strangers and exiles on the earth." These men and women were focused on the future country God had planned for them, and that future country motivated them to live obedient lives.

Knowing that our future is secure in heaven ought to motivate us to live effectively for God on earth.

The same was true for the apostle Paul. He understood that his citizenship was in heaven, yet he was on earth to fulfill God's will. In Philippians 1:21, he wrote, "For to me, to live is Christ and to die is gain." He was saying, "It works out for me either way. As long as I am living, I will do what He wants me to do. But if God decides to take me, it will be better for me." Paul went on to say, "I am hard-pressed from both directions, having the desire to depart and be with Christ, for that is very much better; yet to remain on in the flesh is more necessary for your sake" (vv. 23–24). Paul wanted to go to heaven and be with God, but at the same time, he wanted to stay and fulfill the ministry God had for him on earth.

That is the kind of life God wants us to have—being focused on our future home yet effective in this world until God calls us home.

What are some challenges you are facing today?
In light of these challenges, how can you focus on heaven while remaining effective on earth?

Lord, it is hard to live between two worlds—as a citizen of heaven and a citizen of earth. Help me focus on my future in heaven while being effective on earth until You call me home with You.

Benefits of Being Heavenly Minded

> You do not know what your life will be like tomorrow. You are just a vapor.
>
> —James 4:14

Our future is in heaven, but God has left us in this world—at least for now. Why should we be thinking about heaven while we are still on earth? What difference does a future heaven make in our lives today?

Focusing on heaven reminds us of the brevity of our lives on earth. Both of my parents died at a relatively young age, and while I certainly miss my parents, one of the benefits of their early departure was reminding me of how brief our time here on earth is. It is over in a moment.

Focusing on heaven reminds us of the brevity of our lives on earth.

A few years ago, I talked to somebody who said, "It feels as if God has hit the fast-forward button; things are going so quickly." Have you ever felt that way? James said this about the brevity of life: "You do not know what your life will be like tomorrow. You are just a vapor that appears for a little while and then vanishes away" (James 4:14).

The apostle Peter observed, "All flesh is like grass, and all its glory like the flower of grass. The grass withers, and the flower falls off" (1 Pet. 1:24). As one preacher said, "Life is like grass: it is sown, it is grown, it is mown, it is blown, and then it's gone." Life is over just like that.

King David said it a little more eloquently in Psalm 39:4–5:

> Lord, make me to know my end
> And what is the extent of my days;
> Let me know how transient I am.
> Behold, You have made my days as handbreadths,
> And my lifetime as nothing in Your sight;
> Surely every man at his best is a mere breath.

Focusing on heaven reminds us how short our earthly lives are.

Do you feel as if God has "hit the fast-forward button" in your life? How does the brevity of your earthly life affect your priorities today?

God, help me understand how short my life on earth is. Show me any changes I need to make in my to-do list or priorities so I can make the most of the time You have given me today.

Heaven Helps Us Prepare for Judgment

> Enter through the narrow gate; for the gate is wide and the way is broad that leads to destruction, and there are many who enter through it. For the gate is small and the way is narrow that leads to life, and there are few who find it.
>
> —Matthew 7:13–14

In Matthew 7:13–14, Jesus said, "Enter through the narrow gate; for the gate is wide and the way is broad that leads to destruction, and there are many who enter through it. For the gate is small and the way is narrow that leads to life, and there are few who find it." There is not one road that leads everybody to the same destination. Jesus said there are two roads that lead to two very different destinations.

One road leads to eternal death. Jesus said most people are on that road. Do you know how you can make certain you go to hell when you die? Just do nothing. Keep going the way you are going, and you are guaranteed to end up in hell. We are all born on the road leading away from God.

You say, "How do I get off that road?" Thankfully, there is also a road that leads to eternal life. You have to make a spiritual U-turn to get off the road to hell and get on the narrow road that leads to heaven.

The Bible says the only way you will go to heaven is to get off the road you are on, repent, and put your faith in Jesus to lead you to heaven. The word *repent* means a change of mind that leads to a change of direction. Jesus made that clear in John 14:6: "I am the way, and the truth, and the life; no one comes to the Father but through Me." There are two gates— one that opens to eternal death and one that opens to eternal life.

> *Focusing on heaven prepares us for the certainty of judgment.*

As brief as this life is, the choices we make now impact our eternity forever. Focusing on heaven prepares us for the certainty of judgment.

Which road are you on today: the road to hell or the road to heaven? If you haven't done so already, will you make a spiritual U-turn and put your faith in Jesus?

> *Jesus, thank You for coming to earth to live a perfect life and die on the cross to pay the full penalty for my sins. May I put my faith in You and make choices every day that honor You.*

Heaven Should Affect the Way We Live Today

> Each man's work will become evident; for the day will show it.
>
> —1 Corinthians 3:13

What difference does a future heaven make in our lives today? Focusing on heaven motivates us to live pure lives.

Not long ago, I traveled to another city to preach at a Bible conference. While I was there, I had to tape a national television interview late in the afternoon. All day, I was concerned about how I was going to keep my suit, my tie, and my shirt clean throughout the day until I did that interview. The reason I was concerned about keeping them clean is that I know how unforgiving the bright lights and the HD television camera lens are. They pick up on the tiniest piece of fuzz or dirt, so if I had anything at all on my suit, millions of people would see. I wanted to keep my clothes clean.

Focusing on heaven motivates us to live pure lives.

That is a good illustration of why we want to keep our lives clean. The Bible says that one day our lives, which the Bible compares to spiritual clothes, are going to come under the harsh glare of God's judgment, and He is going to see our lives for what they really are. The Bible says, "Each man's work will become evident; for the day will show it" (1 Cor. 3:13). The Bible often uses clothing as a metaphor for our spiritual lives, and we do not want our lives to become stained by sin and disobedience.

Let's face it: It is hard to keep our lives clean in a polluted world, isn't it? One of the best motivations for keeping your life clean before God is focusing on heaven and your future reunion with Jesus Christ.

———————

Are your spiritual clothes stained by sin and disobedience?

If so, will you take them to Jesus to receive His forgiveness and spiritual cleansing today?

> *Jesus, it's hard to keep my spiritual clothes clean in this polluted world. Forgive me when I give in to temptation and disobey You. Cleanse me from my sin and help me live a pure life for You.*

Heaven Puts Suffering in Perspective

> We look not at the things which are seen, but at the things which are not seen; for the things which are seen are temporal, but the things which are not seen are eternal.
>
> —2 Corinthians 4:18

One of the questions I am often asked is, "Why does God allow suffering and evil in the world?" Many times, when people say that, what they really mean is, "Why does God allow suffering in my life?" Why did God allow me to be fired unfairly? Why did God allow me to suffer through a broken relationship? Why did He allow me to suffer the loss of a loved one?

Interestingly, the Bible never answers the "why" question of suffering. But it does help us put suffering in perspective.

In 2 Corinthians 4:17–18, Paul wrote, "Momentary, light affliction is producing for us an eternal weight of glory far beyond all comparison, while we look not at the things which are seen, but at the things which are not seen; for the things which are seen are temporal, but the things which are not seen are eternal." Paul said his suffering was momentary compared to the eternity of blessing God had planned for him. And the same is true for you.

You may feel as if you are in a situation that will not end. You pray, "God, why don't You stop this?" God understands what you are going through. Whatever problem you are facing is real, and it is heavy to you. But the Bible says that compared to the weight of the blessing God has planned for you for all eternity, it is light. Focusing on heaven does not eliminate suffering, but it does put that suffering in perspective.

Focusing on heaven does not eliminate suffering, but it does put that suffering in perspective.

Although God's promise for heaven is still future, it should affect the way we live every day, for what we do in this life echoes in the halls of heaven forever.

What struggles are you or a loved one going through right now?
In what ways does your eternal future in heaven put that suffering in perspective?

God, I don't understand why You allow evil and suffering, especially in the lives of Your people, but I trust You to work out Your perfect plan. Help me keep suffering in perspective today by focusing on my eternal future in heaven with You.

Is Heaven a Real Place or a State of Mind?

> This Jesus, who has been taken up from you into heaven, will come in just the same way as you have watched Him go into heaven.
>
> —Acts 1:11

One morning in early 1971, John Lennon composed what became the anthem for the ages: "Imagine." In that one-word tribute to utopian ideals, Lennon asked us to imagine what it would be like if there were no heaven.

Where do we go to find out if heaven is a real place or just a figment of our imaginations? Since the Bible is the inspired truth from God, Scripture is the place we turn to find out whether heaven is a real place or a state of mind.

A good place to start in the Bible is with the only person who actually lived in heaven and came to earth to tell us what heaven is like. His name is Jesus Christ. In John 14:2–3, Jesus said, "In My Father's house are many dwelling places; if it were not so, I would have told you; for I go to prepare a place for you. If I go and prepare a place for you, I will come again and receive you to Myself, that where I am, there you may be also."

There are three key words in this passage that help us answer the question, Is heaven a real place or a state of mind? The first Greek word, *topos*, is translated "place." Jesus said three times in this passage: "I go to prepare a *place* for you." Heaven is a place, an exact geographical location. The second word, *mone*, is translated "dwelling places." Jesus said, "In My Father's house are many *dwelling places.*" This word refers to the domicile of a person. Jesus was saying, "In My Father's house, there is a place designed just for you." The third key word is "prepare." Jesus said, "I go to *prepare* a place for you." You do not have to prepare a state of mind.

The Bible assures us that Jesus is in heaven right now, preparing a future residence for us.

The Bible assures us that Jesus is in heaven right now, preparing a future residence for us.

Have you ever thought of heaven as a real place?

Can you imagine what it will be like to live in a place where Jesus is fully present and evil is not?

God, thank You for assuring us in Your Word that heaven is a real place. Whenever this world feels confusing or corrupt, remind me that You are preparing a dwelling place for me that is pleasing and perfect.

Heaven Is a Geographical Location

> This Jesus, who has been taken up from you into heaven, will come in just the same way as you have watched Him go into heaven.
>
> —Acts 1:11

After Jesus rose from the dead, He spent forty days on earth in His new resurrection body. At the end of those forty days, He fulfilled His promise to ascend back to His Father in heaven. Jesus's followers gathered with Him on the Mount of Olives, and Luke recorded what happened:

> He was lifted up while they were looking on, and a cloud received Him out of their sight. And as they were gazing intently into the sky while He was going, behold, two men in white clothing stood beside them. They also said, "Men of Galilee, why do you stand looking into the sky? This Jesus, who has been taken up from you into heaven, will come in just the same way as you have watched Him go into heaven." (Acts 1:9–11)

The book of Acts tells us that Jesus was at the Mount of Olives, and then He ascended into heaven. Can you go from a geographical location into a state of mind? No, that does not make sense. Jesus went from one location, the Mount of Olives, to another location, heaven. The angels said one day Jesus is going to come from heaven, a real

One day Jesus is going to come from heaven, a real location, back to a real place on earth.

28

location, back to a real place on earth. You don't come from a state of mind back to a physical location. Heaven is a geographical location.

The angels told the disciples that Jesus will return "in just the same way." Just as Jesus was literally and visibly brought from earth to heaven, one day Jesus will literally and visibly return from heaven back to earth. And when He comes, "every knee will bow . . . and . . . every tongue will confess that Jesus Christ is Lord, to the glory of God the Father" (Phil. 2:10–11).

———————

Have you bowed your knee to Jesus and confessed with your mouth that He is Lord?

What can you do today to prepare for the literal and visible return of Jesus Christ to earth?

Jesus, I look forward to the day when You will return from heaven back to earth! Help me live today in a way that pleases You.

Where Is Heaven?

> He was lifted up while they were looking on, and a
> cloud received Him out of their sight.
>
> —Acts 1:9

Where is heaven? Can you locate it on a map? The apostle Thomas had that question. After Jesus said, "I am going to prepare a place for you," Thomas asked, "Lord, we do not know where You are going, how do we know the way?" (John 14:5). That is a logical question. Jesus told them they were going to the Father's house—where was that? And how would they get there?

Jesus helped the disciples recalibrate their spiritual GPS. Since they wanted to know how to get to heaven, Jesus said, "I am the way, and the truth, and the life; no one comes to the Father but through Me" (v. 6). In other words, "Do you want to get to My Father's house, this place called heaven? Follow Me."

We have a few clues in the Bible about the location of heaven. First, the Bible seems to indicate that heaven is up. How do we know this? Satan told us so. Now, most of the time Satan is a liar. But kind of like a broken clock is right at least twice a day, Satan is right about a few things.

We have a few clues in the Bible about the location of heaven.

According to Isaiah 14:13, when Satan mounted his rebellion against God, he said, "I will ascend to heaven; I will raise my throne above the stars of God." Wherever the throne of God is, it is up. Satan was saying, "I will ascend to where You are, God." In Acts 1:9, Luke recorded that Jesus "was lifted up while they were looking on, and a cloud received Him out of their sight." Heaven, wherever it is, is up.

Second, the Bible indicates heaven is north. In Isaiah 14:13, Satan also said, "I will sit on the mount of assembly in the recesses of the north." Job 37:22 says, "Out of the north comes golden splendor; around God is awesome majesty." So, in some sense, heaven tends to be north.

Have you ever looked into the sky and tried to see heaven?

In what ways does the Bible's description of heaven as being above us give you hope?

Jesus, thank You for being willing to show us the way to heaven. Every time I look up to the sky, remind me that You will be with me forever in my heavenly home.

Heaven Is a Real Place

> Out of the north comes golden splendor; around God is awesome majesty.
>
> —Job 37:22

Is heaven a place that exists in time and space, even though it may be a gazillion miles away? Is it an actual place in this universe, or is heaven in some other dimension that we cannot even see right now? Is it something like the fifth dimension that Rod Serling used to talk about in *The Twilight Zone*? Is heaven a completely different realm of existence that we can't see or access from earth?

I read with great interest recently that analysts from the Bank of America, one of the most respected financial institutions in the world, say there is up to a 50 percent chance that right now we are living in a computer-generated virtual reality game that was created using artificial intelligence. Now, these are the people who are handling our money. It is kind of a scary thought. I hope I do not make virtual deposits that disappear! These analysts are saying we could be in a computer-generated virtual reality game created with artificial intelligence, and because we are inside the game, we will never know we are inside the game.

Is heaven a completely different realm of existence that we can't see or access from earth?

Some people wonder, "Is heaven like that? Is it in a whole other realm of existence that we cannot see right now?" To answer that question, we need to understand the difference between the present heaven and the future heaven. Thankfully, the Bible gives us important insights that will help us understand what awaits us and our loved ones who are Christians.

What do you think heaven is like? Is it another dimension, like *The Twilight Zone*? Or is it a real place you can travel to? Reflect for a moment about what you imagine heaven to be.

> *God, there are so many things about heaven that I don't understand. Thank You for being gracious to us and providing the answers we need about heaven in Your Word.*

The Present Heaven

> I saw the holy city, new Jerusalem, coming down
> out of heaven from God.
>
> —Revelation 21:2

If you want to understand what awaits you and your loved ones who are Christians in heaven, then you need to understand the difference between the present heaven and the future heaven.

The Bible talks about three current "heavens." The first heaven is earth's atmosphere. It's where the birds and jetliners fly. The second heaven is outer space, where the stars, planets, and galaxies exist. And there is a third heaven right now that is the abode of God. This third heaven is where God is, the presence of God.

In 2 Corinthians 12:2–4, the apostle Paul said that he had an experience in which he was caught up into the third heaven and saw marvelous things, and then he came back to earth. This experience made a profound impact on his life. Paul was caught up to the third heaven, where God is.

The moment a Christian dies, he or she goes to be in the presence of God.

This third heaven is the place you and I go when we die. If you are a Christian, you go into the abode of God. The Bible says that for a Christian, "to be absent from the body [is] to be at home with the Lord" (2 Cor. 5:8). The moment a Christian dies, he or she goes to be in the presence of God.

But that is the present heaven. Even though we Christians go to be with God immediately after we die, that is not our permanent eternal dwelling place. Our final residence is not up there; it is down here on the earth. The Bible explains that there is a future heaven—a fourth heaven, if you will—that God is preparing for us right now.

What comes to your mind when you think about the word *home*? What do you think it will feel like to be "at home" with the Lord?

Lord, thank You for assuring me in Your Word that the moment I die, I will be in Your presence. Whenever I am tempted to worry about my inevitable death, I will choose instead to look forward to the time when I will be "at home" with You.

The Future Heaven

> I saw the holy city, new Jerusalem, coming down out of heaven from God, made ready as a bride adorned for her husband.
>
> —Revelation 21:2

There is a future heaven that Jesus is constructing for us right now. In John 14:2–3, Jesus said He was going to be with the Father to prepare a place for you and me.

Right now, we are waiting for the next great event on God's prophetic timetable—the rapture of the church, when all believers who are alive will be caught up to meet the Lord in the third heaven, where God is right now. The rapture will be followed by the tribulation, when God pours out His judgment on the world. The climax of the great tribulation will be the battle of Armageddon and the return of Jesus Christ to earth. Jesus will reign on earth for a thousand years, called the millennium. The earth is improved, but it is not re-created at that time. At the end of the thousand years, all unbelievers are judged at the great white throne judgment and cast into the lake of fire. Then the fire of God's judgment destroys the present heaven and earth.

There is a future heaven that Jesus is constructing for us right now.

In Revelation 21:1–2, the apostle John said,

> I saw a new heaven [the future heaven] and a new earth; for the first heaven and the first earth passed away, and there is

no longer any sea. And I saw the holy city, new Jerusalem, coming down out of heaven from God, made ready as a bride adorned for her husband.

The future heaven that Jesus is creating for us will come out of the current heaven and rest on the newly re-created earth. That is our permanent home.

Perhaps the concept of the present heaven (where we go immediately after we die) and this future heaven is a bit confusing to you. Let me illustrate it this way: Let's say you retire and move to the city where your children live. You buy a piece of land to construct the home of your dreams. While that construction project is going on, you need a place to live, so you rent an apartment. The apartment is comfortable, but it is not your permanent dwelling place. The same thing is true for Christians when we die. When we die, right now, we go into the presence of God. We are aware, and we are with our loved ones, but it is a temporary place. God is building a permanent home for us.

What are some things you would change about your current home? How does God's promise of your future home in heaven give you comfort during times of change or anxiety?

God, thank You for building a permanent home for me, where I will be in Your presence forever. When things or relationships in my earthly home feel broken, help me rest in the hope of my eternal, perfect home with You.

The Future Heaven Will Be New

> Behold, I create new heavens and a new earth; and the former things will not be remembered or come to mind.
>
> —Isaiah 65:17

What will heaven be like? Let's look at some characteristics of this future heaven that will be our eternal home.

The apostle John said our future home will be new. In Revelation 21:1, John wrote, "I saw a new heaven and a new earth; for the first heaven and the first earth passed away, and there is no longer any sea." After the millennium—the thousand years after Jesus's second coming, when Jesus Christ will reign on earth—there will be a great destruction of the present heaven and earth. They will pass away.

The apostle John said our future home will be new.

The apostle Peter told us about the burning up of the present heaven and earth as well. In 2 Peter 3:7, he said, "By His word the present heavens and earth are being reserved for fire, kept for the day of judgment and destruction of ungodly men." He continued, "But the day of the Lord will come like a thief, in which the heavens will pass away with a roar and the elements will be destroyed with intense heat, and the earth and its works will be burned up" (v. 10).

What is this fire of judgment that is coming to destroy the earth? It's an intense heat, because even the elements, the basic building blocks of this world, will be completely destroyed. Some have speculated that perhaps it is a nuclear holocaust that comes at the end of the great tribulation.

The truth is, we do not know exactly how God will accomplish this, but everything you see around you, everything you have accumulated, and everything you have set your affections on in this world will one day be completely burned up.

Why is it sometimes necessary to get rid of an old thing in order to replace it with a new version?

How does 2 Peter 3:10 affect your perspective on the things you are accumulating in this world?

Lord, help me develop a healthy perspective on material things and accolades in this world. Show me how to be diligent without focusing too much on things that will someday be burned up and replaced with something new.

Why Will God Destroy This Earth?

> Through one man sin entered into the world, and death through sin, and so death spread to all men, because all sinned.
>
> —Romans 5:12

Why is it important for God to completely destroy this present heaven and earth? Why can't He just do a little renovation project of this earth, maybe add a few upgrades?

The Bible says there is one reason God has to destroy everything around us. It is a three-letter word: *sin*. Sin has infected and ruined everything in this world. The reason you and I have to have a new body to enter heaven is that our current bodies have been infected with sin. Romans 5:12 says, "Through one man sin entered into the world, and death through sin, and so death spread to all men, because all sinned." You have to have a new body for eternity. If you are a Christian, then you are going to have a sin-free body.

Everything about this world has been infected with sin.

Just as our bodies have been infected by sin, this world has also been infected with sin. Everything about this world has been infected with sin. Romans 8:22 says, "The whole creation groans" in anticipation. The whole direction of everything in this world is downward. Everything is deteriorating because we have been infected with the sin virus. But God is going to remove that for the new heaven and earth, and all of it will be a fulfillment of Isaiah 65:17: "Behold, I create new heavens and a new earth; and the former things will not be remembered or come to mind."

In the new heaven, our eternal place, we will not be disembodied spirits. Once we die, we inhabit a new body. We are created to be physical beings as well as spiritual beings. Since we are physical beings, we need a physical location in which to live for eternity.

What are some of the negative effects of sin that you can observe in our world?

How does the Bible's promise of a new, sin-free world give you hope?

God, whenever I experience the negative effects of sin in my life, help me remember that You are preparing a new heaven and a new earth—a place where sin will be no more.

What Will Heaven Be Like?

> He will wipe away every tear from their eyes; and there will no longer be any death; there will no longer be any mourning, or crying, or pain.
>
> —Revelation 21:4

What will heaven be like? The Bible says that heaven is going to be familiar to us.

You may not like the idea of moving to an unfamiliar destination. But heaven is going to be a familiar place because it is going to be this world, not some other world, in which we will live for eternity. In Revelation 21:4, John said, "He will wipe away every tear from their eyes; and there will no longer be any death; there will no longer be any mourning, or crying, or pain."

Heaven will have no oceans. Revelation 21:1 says, "I saw a new heaven and a new earth; for the first heaven and the first earth passed away, and there is no longer any sea."

The new heaven will have no sun or moon. Revelation 21:23 says, "The city has no need of the sun or of the moon to shine on it, for the glory of God has illumined it, and its lamp is the Lamb."

Heaven will be free from sin. Revelation 22:3 says, "There will no longer be any curse." Furthermore, everybody will know the Lord at that time. Habakkuk 2:14 says, "The earth will be filled with the knowledge of the glory of the LORD, as the waters cover the sea."

Heaven will have a capital. The centerpiece is the new Jerusalem. Revelation 3:12 calls Jerusalem "the city of My God." Revelation 21:2 says, "I saw the holy city, new Jerusalem, coming down out of heaven from God, made ready as a bride adorned for her husband." It will be unlike any city we have ever seen. In the new Jerusalem, there will be no house of worship, because God and His Son will represent the temple of God. And in God's presence, we will live, work, play, and worship Him forever.

> *God is creating heaven right now with you in mind.*

The Bible says Jesus is in heaven preparing a place for you. The greatest thing about that are the words *for you*. God is creating heaven right now with you in mind. The place God is preparing for you is beyond your wildest imagination. Don't you want to go?

Do you want to go to heaven someday?
What will you do today to prepare your heart to live in heaven for eternity?

God, thank You for creating heaven right now with me in mind! I look forward to the day when I will live, work, play, and worship You in Your presence forever.

Have Some People Already Visited Heaven?

He has also set eternity in [our] heart.
—Ecclesiastes 3:11

"God is calling me." Those were the final words spoken by evangelist Dwight L. Moody on December 22, 1899, when he died at his home in Northfield, Massachusetts. Of course, the fact that D. L. Moody died is nothing unusual. We all die, don't we? But what was interesting about Moody's experience is what happened immediately before his death. According to an article in the *New York Times*, right before he died, Moody said, "I see earth receding; heaven is opening; God is calling me."[1]

Did Moody have what we call today a "near-death experience"? His great-nephew Raymond Moody apparently thinks so. Raymond Moody is the father of the modern "near-death experience" fad. He wrote a bestselling book called *Life After Life*, which describes countless people who had an out-of-body experience when they were near death in which they visited the other side and were able to come back and relate what they had seen. These experiences differ from the experience of D. L. Moody in two significant ways. First, D. L. Moody actually died. He did not nearly die. Second, he never came back to share what he saw on the other side.

That brings up an interesting question: Have some people who are alive right now already visited heaven? How do we make sense of the books written by people who say, "We went to the other side. We saw what God has prepared for us, and we have come back to tell you all about it"?

The International Association for Near-Death Studies defines a *near-death experience* as "a profound psy-

Have some people who are alive right now already visited heaven?

chological event that may occur to a person close to death or if not near death in a situation of physical or emotional crisis, and it includes transcendental and mystical elements."[2] Many people claim to have had these experiences, but are they valid?

Why do you think people are fascinated by near-death experiences? What near-death stories are you familiar with?

Lord, I'm glad You are in control of my life, my death, and my eternal life! Help me look forward with anticipation to the day when I, too, will see earth receding and heaven opening for me to join You forever.

Why Are Stories about Near-Death Experiences So Popular?

> Do not believe every spirit, but test the spirits to see whether they are from God.
>
> —1 John 4:1

Many people have claimed to have had a near-death experience. Whether these experiences are valid or not, nobody can deny their popularity. Books by these people have sold in the millions. Why are we so fascinated by this?

First, we are naturally curious about the unknown. There is a dark curtain that is drawn between this life and the next life. It is a mystery to us in many ways what awaits us on the other side, and it is only natural that we would want to know what happens after our few years here on earth.

No matter how well-intentioned or godly somebody is, we need to test their experience against the truth of God's Word.

Second, the popularity of near-death experiences is partly due to our longing for heaven. Ecclesiastes 3:11 says that God "has also set eternity in [our] heart." We all have a desire to know what God is preparing for us after we leave this earth. We know there is more to life than what we are experiencing right now.

So, where do we turn to find answers about what God has prepared for us?

Whenever we come to think about a near-death experience, we need to examine it in light of what the Bible says. In 1 John 4:1, the apostle John warned, "Do not believe every spirit, but test the spirits to see whether they are from God, because many false prophets have gone out into the world." No matter how well-intentioned or godly somebody is, we need to test their experience against the truth of God's Word.

In Acts 17, the Bereans listened to the preaching of the apostle Paul. Verse 11 says the Bereans "received the word with great eagerness, examining the Scriptures daily to see whether these things were so." These godly men and women heard the testimony of Paul, and then they searched the Scriptures to see if these things were true or not. Whenever you hear about someone's experience with God, every word needs to be tested by the truth of God's Word.

Why is it important to test all spiritual matters against the truth of God's Word?

In what ways is the Bible more reliable than someone's experience?

God, You have set eternity in my heart, and I long to know about heaven. Give me opportunities to study the Bible, so I can examine everything I hear according to what You have said.

Are Near-Death Experiences Valid?

It is appointed for men to die once and after this comes judgment.

—Hebrews 9:27

Are near-death experiences valid? How do we know that these experiences are not simply chemical reactions produced by the brain in times of stress that can lead to the sensation of light? Some of these chemicals can also give the sensation of an out-of-body experience. On the other hand, if a near-death experience leads somebody to faith in Christ or causes them to make positive changes in their lives, who are we to deny that their experience is real?

We need to examine all accounts of near-death experiences in the light of Scripture. First, near death is not death. The Bible is very clear on this point. You only die once. Hebrews 9:27

The only way we know about heaven is from what God has recorded in His book, the Bible.

says, "It is appointed for men to die once and after this comes judgment." You may say, "What about Lazarus? What about Jairus's daughter? What about those cases where God raised people from the dead?" We have a

word to describe those events: *miracles*. The reason we call them miracles is because they are the exception to the rule; they are not the rule.

Not once in the Bible did somebody whom God raised from the dead ever tell about what they saw on the other side. The only people who can tell us with accuracy what is in heaven are those who have been to heaven, and you have to be dead to get to heaven. The only way we know about heaven is from what God has recorded in His book, the Bible.

What is the difference between death and near death?

How does Hebrews 9:27 apply to stories of people who say they died and returned to tell us about it?

Lord Jesus, I know that Your Word is more reliable than any so-called near-death experience. Open my eyes to the lies of this world and guide me to the truth of Your Word.

The Bible Is Sufficient

> All Scripture is inspired by God and profitable for teaching, for reproof, for correction, for training in righteousness; so that the man of God may be adequate, equipped for every good work.
>
> —2 Timothy 3:16–17

The presupposition behind books written by Christians about near-death experiences is this: "The Bible is good, but it is not sufficient. There is more information God wants us to have about heaven, and He has given me that information to share with you for $22.95."

But look at what the apostle Paul said about the sufficiency of God's Word:

> We do not want you to be uninformed, brethren, about those who are asleep [Christians who have died], so that you will not grieve as do the rest who have no hope. For if we believe that Jesus died and rose again, even so God will bring with Him those who have fallen asleep in Jesus. (1 Thess. 4:13–14)

During the last thirty-five years, I have conducted hundreds of funeral services. And every time I conduct a funeral service, I read this passage of Scripture in 1 Thessalonians 4. I also read Revelation 21:4, which says, "He will wipe away every tear from their eyes; and there will no longer be any death; there will no longer be any mourning, or crying, or pain; the first things have passed away." I have never felt the need to reach into some secular book to give additional information about heaven.

Every time I read those verses and look into the eyes of those sitting in the front two rows who have lost a loved one, I see God's Word bringing comfort and peace to them. That is the power of God's Word. God's Word is sufficient. We do not need any extrabiblical revelation about heaven.

> *God's Word is sufficient. We do not need any extrabiblical revelation about heaven.*

Have you lost a loved one to death?

What comfort or encouragement do these Bible passages provide to those who are grieving?

> *God, I look forward to the day when You will wipe every tear from my eyes and there will be no more mourning or pain. May I share the hope of heaven with those who need encouragement today.*

Principles to Evaluate
Near-Death Experiences

Satan disguises himself as an angel of light.
—2 Corinthians 11:14

Are near-death experiences valid? The Bible gives us principles to evaluate these experiences.

First, adding to or taking away from the Bible is condemned by God. The best explanation of heaven is found in the book of Revelation. After John received this revelation, he said,

> I testify to everyone who hears the words of the prophecy of this book: if anyone adds to them, God will add to him the plagues which are written in this book; and if anyone takes away from the words of the book of this prophecy, God will take away his part from the tree of life and from the holy city, which are written in this book. (Rev. 22:18–19)

Anyone who says, "God has given me a revelation about what heaven is like," is treading on dangerous ground by adding to what God has revealed in the Bible.

Next, we should question the identity of any being of light. Many people who have had a near-death experience claim to have met God, angels, or some undefined deity. Some even claim to have seen Jesus, but the message that Jesus supposedly gave them contradicts Scripture. People have said, "I saw Jesus, and He told me all people are welcomed into heaven." Yet Hebrews 13:8 says, "Jesus Christ is the same yesterday and today and forever." The Jesus in heaven does not contradict what Jesus said on earth. We need to be careful of any so-called being of light who gives a message that contradicts Scripture. Jesus said there is one way to heaven, and it is through faith in Him.

We need to take seriously the warning of 1 Timothy 4:1: "In later times some will fall away from the faith, paying attention to deceitful spirits and doctrines of demons." I believe some of these experiences are demonic. When people say they saw a light and a divine being telling them everyone is going to heaven, I believe them, but the bright light they saw was not God. In 2 Corinthians 11:14, Paul said, "Satan disguises himself as an angel of light." He is deceiving people into what awaits them on the other side.

> *We need to be careful of any so-called being of light who gives a message that contradicts Scripture.*

Why does God condemn adding to or taking away from the Bible?

Have you ever considered that descriptions of a "being of light" might be Satan or his demons?

How does this affect your perspective on some near-death experiences?

Lord Jesus, You are the same yesterday and today and forever, and Your gospel of salvation through faith in You will never change. Protect me from the deception of the evil one.

Are Near-Death Experiences Biblical?

> [Paul] was caught up into Paradise and heard in-expressible words, which a man is not permitted to speak.
>
> —2 Corinthians 12:4

Are near-death experiences biblical? Let's examine these experiences in the light of Scripture.

Consider this: Jesus's death and resurrection are central to any revelation from God. Some people think Paul had a near-death experience on the road to Damascus (Acts 9:3–6). But this was not a near-death experience. First, Paul was very much alive when this happened to him. Second, the light Paul saw was not some metaphysical light; it was a real light that blinded him for days. Third, when Paul told this account to King Agrippa, he never gave any description that resembled a near-death experience. Finally, Jesus gave Paul the mission of preaching the message of salvation through Him, not some feel-good message that says everybody is going to heaven.

The Bible does not record any near-death experiences. There are biblical accounts of God raising people from the dead, but none of these people told about what they saw on the other side. Consider the apostle Paul, who said that he "was caught up to the third heaven" (2 Cor. 12:2). The third heaven is the abode of God. What did Paul see? He said he was "not permitted to speak" about his experience (v. 4). Think about that. Paul wrote over half of the New Testament. If God wanted us to have a complete description of what heaven was like, don't you think He would have entrusted that revelation to Paul? But God said, "Do not write it down."

Why has God restricted the information we have about heaven? I think what is in store for us is so magnificent that human words only diminish the glory of heaven. I also think if we knew what was awaiting us, we could not wait to get out of here. That is why Paul, who had seen heaven, was able to say, "For to me, to live is Christ and to die is gain" (Phil. 1:21). Very simply, there are no biblical accounts of near-death experiences.

God can do whatever He wants to do, but the weight of evidence is against near-death experiences.

God can do whatever He wants to do, but the weight of evidence is against near-death experiences. Everything we need to know about our eternal home is found in the Bible.

How does the knowledge that the Bible doesn't record any near-death experiences affect your perspective on near-death stories?

Lord, thank You for telling me everything I need to know about heaven in the Bible. Protect me from being deceived by the enemy's tactics to distract me from the truth of Your Word.

There Is One Fate for All

> It is the same for all. There is one fate for the righteous and for the wicked; for the good, for the clean and for the unclean; for the man who offers a sacrifice and for the one who does not sacrifice.
>
> —Ecclesiastes 9:2

While it is true that there are certain things about the afterlife that we cannot know for sure, one thing is crystal clear: we are all going to die one day, and when that happens, we are going to one of two eternal destinations: heaven or hell.

In his book *Heaven*, Randy Alcorn observed that "worldwide, 3 people die every second, 180 every minute, and nearly 11,000 every hour. If the Bible is right about what happens to us after death, it means that more than 250,000 people every day go either to Heaven or to Hell."[1] That blows our minds, doesn't it? A quarter of a million spirits depart the earth every single day, bound for one of two eternal destinies. Numbers like this prove the accuracy of the old adage: "No one gets out of this world alive."

There is one fate, but there are two different destinations: heaven and hell.

Why is death inevitable for every one of us? Why does no one get out of this world alive? In Ecclesiastes 9:2, Solomon said, "It is the same for all. There is one fate for the righteous and for the wicked; for the good, for the clean and for the unclean; for the man who offers a sacrifice and for the one who does not sacrifice." It does not matter whether you are good, bad, righteous, unrighteous, a believer, or an unbeliever, there is one fate for everybody: death. We are all going to die. There is one fate, but there are two different destinations: heaven and hell.

Have you come to terms with the fact that you are going to die one day? How does the inevitability of your death affect the way you live today?

Heavenly Father, help me make the most of my time today, knowing that my time on this earth is limited. May I spend today, and every day, seeking Your glory and fulfilling Your plan for my life.

Why Do People Have to Die?

The wages of sin is death.
—Romans 6:23

Why do both Christians and non-Christians have to die? It is because of the virus of sin we have all inherited. Romans 3:23 says, "All have sinned and fall short of the glory of God." Romans 6:23 says, "The wages of sin is death." Not only is death inevitable because of sin but it also brings its own kind of terror to all of us. In Job 18:14, Job called death "the king of terrors." The psalmist said, "My heart is in anguish within me, and the terrors of death have fallen upon me" (55:4). Death is a nightmare for those who die without faith in Jesus Christ.

Death is a nightmare for those who die without faith in Jesus Christ.

A few years ago, actor Jack Nicholson was in a movie called *The Bucket List*. This movie was about two men with terminal cancer who decided to do everything on their list of things they wanted to do before they kicked the bucket. In an interview, Nicholson said making that movie was transformational in his own life. He said:

> I used to live so freely. The mantra for my generation was "Be your own man!" I always said, "Hey, you can have whatever rules you want—I'm going to have mine. I'll accept the guilt. I'll pay the check. I'll do the time." I chose my own way. That was my philosophical position well into my 50s. As I've gotten

older, I've had to adjust. . . . We all want to go on forever, don't we? We fear the unknown. Everybody goes to that wall, yet nobody knows what's on the other side. That's why we fear death.[1]

Why do you think people are afraid of dying?

What would you say to encourage someone who fears death?

Heavenly Father, dying can be scary, especially when I consider the inevitability of my own death. When I feel afraid, help me trust in You and give me Your peace that passes understanding.

Our Fear of Death

> Since the children share in flesh and blood, He Himself likewise also partook of the same, that through death He might render powerless him who had the power of death, that is, the devil, and might free those who through fear of death were subject to slavery all their lives.
>
> —Hebrews 2:14–15

It is understandable for unbelievers to fear death—they don't know what awaits them on the other side of the grave. But if we are honest, many Christians also fear death because of the unknown.

The prospect of dying can be unnerving. What happens to Christians when we die? Do we cease to exist? Do we go to sleep for a thousand years, awaiting a future resurrection? Do we go into a waiting place, hoping somebody will pray hard enough or give enough money to get us out? Without a doubt, the thought of death can fill us with terror and dread. However, knowing our destination when we depart this life can dramatically diminish that understandable fear.

Death is not the end. It is just the beginning of our eternal reunion with God.

One of my mentors in seminary used to admonish us to make heaven the center of our preaching. He would say, "We are not in the land of the living headed to the land of the dying. Instead, we are in the land of the dying on our way to the land of the living." And that is true for a Christian. Death is not the end. It is just the beginning of our eternal reunion with God. That is what awaits Christians when we die.

To understand what happens to a Christian when he or she dies, it is important that we distinguish between the present heaven and the future heaven. The present heaven is where God is right now, and that is where we go the moment we die. We go into the presence of God, but that is not our eternal dwelling place. In John 14:2–3, Jesus said that He is in that present heaven preparing a new place for us. Heaven, where God is, is already prepared, but Jesus is working on a new location for us.

Have you ever thought of death as a beginning, not an end?
How does this perspective affect the way you feel about death?

> *Jesus, thank You for preparing a place for me in heaven. May I look forward in anticipation, not fear, to the day when I will pass through the gate of death into an eternity with You.*

Where Do Christians Go When They Die?

Today you shall be with Me in Paradise.
—Luke 23:43

John said in Revelation 21:2, "I saw the holy city, new Jerusalem, coming down out of heaven from God." The new Jerusalem that Jesus is preparing for us will descend out of the current heaven and reside on a re-created earth. That is our ultimate, future destination as believers. But the moment Christians die, we immediately depart from this world into the presence of God. There is no soul sleep. A Christian goes immediately into the presence of God. How do I know that?

The moment Christians die, we immediately depart from this world into the presence of God.

Look at what Scripture says about the immediacy of our entrance into God's presence. In Luke 23:43, Jesus said to the thief on the cross who had just exercised faith, "Today you shall be with Me in Paradise." And in Acts 7:59, "Stephen . . . called on the Lord and said, 'Lord Jesus, receive my spirit!'"

The seminal passage in the Bible that describes what happens to Christians when they die is 2 Corinthians 5:1. In this passage, the apostle Paul said that if our earthly body is torn down, then we have a body from God that is eternal. Paul said our bodies are like a tent. Who wants to live in a tent for eternity? Our bodies are a temporary dwelling, a tent that will be put away one day.

Then Paul said in verse 6, "While we are at home in the body we are absent from the Lord." We cannot be in two locations at once. As long as we are here, we cannot also be in heaven with God. That is what Paul was saying. We think this world is our home, but it is not. It is a temporary location. Yes, we have people we love here. Yes, God has given us an assignment here. But it is temporary. As long as we are here, we are not at home with the Lord.

———

Why is it important to know that we enter God's presence immediately after death?

How does thinking of your current body as a temporary tent help you look forward to heaven?

Lord, there are many wonderful things in this world, but this is not my home. Help me to be faithful to fulfill Your assignment for me here until I am able to join You in my heavenly home.

Forever at Home with the Lord

We are of good courage, I say, and prefer rather to be absent from the body and to be at home with the Lord.

—2 Corinthians 5:8

In 2 Corinthians 5:8, the apostle Paul said, "We are of good courage, I say, and prefer rather to be absent from the body and to be at home with the Lord." He was saying, "I prefer to be once-for-all absent from the body so that I can be once-for-all at home with the Lord." That is what happens to Christians when we die. The moment we leave this body, we are forever at home with the Lord.

When you die, your spirit goes to be with the Lord awaiting the final resurrection body you will receive at the rapture. In 1 Thessalonians 4:16, Paul said, "The Lord Himself will descend from heaven with a shout, with the voice of the archangel and with the trumpet of God, and the dead in Christ will rise first."

The moment we leave this body, we are forever at home with the Lord.

Who are the dead in Christ? They are Christians who have already died. Their spirits are in heaven and their bodies are in the ground, but at the rapture, their bodies will be raised. Then that generation of believers who are alive at that time will also be caught up, and together they will meet the Lord in the air. The Lord will descend; you and I who are in heaven with God will descend.

In 1 Corinthians 15:52, the apostle Paul said at that moment, "in the twinkling of an eye . . . the dead will be raised imperishable, and we will be changed." At the rapture of the church, Christians will receive brand-new bodies that are forever free from suffering and death.

———————

How does the knowledge that immediately after you die, you will be "at home with the Lord" give you "good courage"?

Lord Jesus, thank You for preparing the place where I will be forever at home with You. I look forward to receiving a brand-new body that is free from suffering and death!

How Were Old Testament Saints Saved?

> [Abraham] believed in the Lord; and He reckoned it to him as righteousness.
>
> —Genesis 15:6

We know that when Christians die, they are immediately ushered into the presence of Jesus Christ. The apostle Paul made it clear in 2 Corinthians 5:8 that "to be absent from the body" is "to be at home with the Lord." But what about those who died before Jesus came? What happened to the Old Testament saints like Abraham, David, and Jeremiah? Where did they go when they died?

It is an interesting question. Were the Old Testament saints even saved? If so, how? They lived before Jesus offered His sacrifice. There is a very simple answer: People in the Old Testament were saved the same way you and I are saved. They were saved by the death of Jesus Christ on the cross for their sins.

All believers— whether they lived before Christ or after Christ—are saved the same way: by the death of Jesus Christ.

How could Jesus's death save men and women who lived before Jesus? They were saved on credit. Genesis 15:6 says that Abraham "believed in the Lord; and He reckoned it to him as righteousness." Abraham and other Old Testament saints believed what God revealed to them, and their exercise of their faith allowed them to be saved on credit. The bill for their sins, just like the bill for our sins, came due on Mount Calvary, and Jesus paid that debt for all of us. That is why He said, "It is finished!" (John 19:30).

All believers—whether they lived before Christ or after Christ—are saved the same way: by the death of Jesus Christ.

Why is it important to understand that salvation has always been through faith in Jesus Christ?

How will you share that good news with someone today?

> *Jesus, thank You for shedding Your blood on the cross to pay my sin debt and make a way for me to live forever in Your presence. May I live today in light of my sure and certain salvation through faith in You.*

Where Did Old Testament Saints Go When They Died?

> The poor man died and was carried away by the angels to Abraham's bosom.
>
> —Luke 16:22

Where did the Old Testament saints go when they died? To understand where they went, we need to look at two important biblical terms that refer to the place of the dead: the Hebrew word *sheol* and the Greek word *hades*. Both words mean roughly the same thing: "covered" or "hidden." According to some scholars, *sheol* is divided into two compartments: Paradise (or "Abraham's bosom") where the righteous reside, and a place of torment called hades where the unrighteous reside.

In Luke 16, Jesus told a story of two men who died. One was a poor man named Lazarus. When Lazarus died, he went to Abraham's bosom because he trusted in God. The other man in Jesus's story was a rich man who died and went to hades, a place of suffering. Jesus said,

> The poor man died and was carried away by the angels to Abraham's bosom; and the rich man also died and was buried. In Hades he lifted up his eyes, being in torment, and saw Abraham far away and Lazarus in his bosom. And he cried out and said, "Father Abraham, have mercy on me, and send Lazarus so that he may dip the tip of his finger in water and cool off my tongue, for I am in agony in this flame." (vv. 22–24)

This passage reminds us of a couple of things. First of all, not everyone goes to the same location when they die. Jesus said there is a place of blessing and there is a place of judgment. Second, this passage reminds us that when we die, we immediately begin experiencing either God's blessing or God's wrath. There is not a waiting time. Immediately, Lazarus was welcomed to Abraham's presence (or "bosom") and began experiencing the blessings God had for him. Immediately, the rich man was in hades, a place of torment.

When the Old Testament saints died, they went into the presence of the Lord.

I believe that when the Old Testament saints died, they went into the presence of the Lord. Believers go immediately into God's presence, where we await the creation of the new heaven and new earth that will be our permanent destination.

What are some differences between Abraham's bosom and hades? How does Luke 16 help you understand the two different experiences for those who die?

God, no amount of possessions or accomplishments in this life can affect where I spend eternity—only my faith in Jesus Christ. Thank You for Your forgiveness, which enables me to experience the blessings You have for me in heaven.

Where Do Unbelievers Go When They Die?

This is the second death, the lake of fire. And if anyone's name was not found written in the book of life, he was thrown into the lake of fire.

—Revelation 20:14–15

What happens to unbelievers when they die? Just as believers have a current destination (the third heaven) and a future destination (the new heaven and new earth), so there is a temporary and eternal destination for the unsaved. The unsaved immediately go to a place called hades.

Luke 16:23–24 says,

In Hades [the rich man] lifted up his eyes, being in torment, and saw Abraham far away and Lazarus in his bosom. And he cried out and said, "Father Abraham, have mercy on me, and send Lazarus so that he may dip the tip of his finger in water and cool off my tongue, for I am in agony in this flame."

Hades is the temporary waiting place of the unsaved dead. It is a place of torment that begins the moment an unbeliever dies. That is where the unbelievers go right now, but that is not their final destination.

The final destination for unbelievers is the lake of fire. In Revelation 20:12–15, John said,

I saw the dead, the great and the small, standing before the throne, and books were opened; and another book was opened, which is the book of life; and the dead were judged from the things which were written in the books, according to their deeds. And the sea gave up the dead which were in it, and death and Hades gave up the dead which were in them; and they were judged, every one of them according to their deeds. Then death and Hades were thrown into the lake of fire.

The final destination for unbelievers is the lake of fire.

This is the second death, the lake of fire. And if anyone's name was not found written in the book of life, he was thrown into the lake of fire.

The lake of fire is a place of forever suffering.

What are some words the rich man used to describe hades in Luke 16? How does his description help you understand what it is like to be away from the presence of God?

God, thank You that my name is written in Your book of life because I trusted in Jesus Christ as my Savior. As I reflect on the sobering reality of the lake of fire, give me the opportunity to share the gospel with unbelievers today.

Heaven and Hell Are Eternal Choices

> In Hades [the rich man] lifted up his eyes, being
> in torment.
>
> —Luke 16:23

When unbelievers die, they go immediately to a terrible place called hades. The common experience in both the temporary location, hades, and the ultimate place for the unsaved, the lake of fire, is physical pain. In the story Jesus told in Luke 16:24, the rich man who was in hades said he was "in agony" because of "this flame."

Right now, those who die without Christ are in hades awaiting their final judgment, the great white throne judgment. At that judgment, hades will be emptied and all the unsaved who have ever lived will stand before God. And because their names are not written in the Lamb's book of life, they will be judged by their deeds. That is a choice they made in this life. On that day, all unbelievers will see that their works do not meet the standard of perfect righteousness that God requires and understand why they have been sentenced to the lake of fire.

Hell and heaven are forever choices.

Here is the basic truth everyone needs to understand: when we die, we immediately begin experiencing God's blessing or God's judgment. While it is true that at some future day believers will change location from the third heaven to the new heaven and new earth, and unbelievers will also change location from hades into the lake of fire, a change of location is not the same as a change of eternal destiny.

If you wait until you die to choose your destination, then you will have waited one second too long. Hell and heaven are forever choices.

Have you made the "forever choice" of heaven by putting your faith in Jesus Christ?

How does the great white throne judgment affect your attitude toward your salvation?

How does it affect your attitude toward unbelievers?

> *God, the reality of Your judgment of unbelievers makes me grateful for Your grace! Thank You for saving me and securing my eternity in heaven. Help me pray for my unbelieving friends and invite them to join me in heaven by putting their faith in Jesus Christ.*

What Will We Do in Heaven?

> Worthy is the Lamb that was slain to receive power
> and riches and wisdom and might and honor and
> glory and blessing.
>
> —Revelation 5:12

Many people, even Christians, have fallen for the myth that heaven is going to be a place of perpetual boredom populated by boring people. But nothing could be further from the truth! People who believe that heaven is boring do so because they have embraced certain myths about God, heaven, and eternity.

Some people believe the myth that God is a cosmic killjoy. They think He is a perennial party pooper, and Satan is the life of the party. Those who have come to that conclusion are convinced that heaven will be as dull as watching paint dry, while hell will be as exhilarating as a NASCAR race. But both of those conclusions are based on a flawed understanding of Satan and God.

Have you ever been stuck at a dinner party, seated next to a hopelessly boring person? Minutes drag on like hours, and you are convinced the evening will never end. Satan is that kind of companion. Did you know there is nothing interesting about Satan? He never created anything; instead he ruined everything. Satan is per-

If you want to know how exciting God is, just look around you at everything He has created.

petually boring and completely unoriginal. Who would want to be stuck with him for eternity?

Contrast that to God. If you want to know how exciting God is, just look around you at everything He has created. Everything we live in and watch is good, beautiful, enjoyable, refreshing, fascinating, and exciting because it was created by Someone who is all of those things.

Why do you think Satan tries to deceive people with the myth that heaven will be boring?

What would you say to someone who believes that God is a "cosmic killjoy"?

God, You are the Creator of all things in this world, and Your creation is fascinating, unique, and beautiful! I can only imagine how much more exciting and joyful heaven will be.

Heaven Is Not Boring

> Every created thing which is in heaven and on the
> earth and under the earth and on the sea, and all
> things in them, I heard saying, "To Him who sits
> on the throne, and to the Lamb, be blessing and
> honor and glory and dominion forever and ever."
> —Revelation 5:13

Some people mistakenly believe that heaven will be monotonous. The fact is, no matter how good something is, we get bored with it after a while, don't we? So we suppose that even as good as heaven is, if we do the same thing over and over and over again, it has to be boring.

But the problem isn't heaven; the problem is us. A friend of mine used to tell her children whenever they complained of being bored that "only boring people get bored." It wasn't that my friend's kids didn't have enough to do—they had a house full of video games, televisions, movies, board games, sports equipment, pets, and friends. They just got tired of doing the same things every day. It is ironic that any child (or adult for that matter) in America could play with thousands of dollars' worth of video equipment and be more bored with life than a child in an impoverished country playing with two sticks and a stone.

The problem isn't heaven; the problem is us.

Monotony does not have to be boring. G. K. Chesterton made this observation:

A child kicks his legs rhythmically through excess, not absence, of life. Because children have abounding vitality, because they are in spirit fierce and free, therefore they want things repeated and unchanged. They always say, "Do it again"; and the grown-up person does it again until he is nearly dead. For grown-up people are not strong enough to exult in monotony. But perhaps God is strong enough to exult in monotony. It is possible that God says every morning, "Do it again" to the sun; and every evening, "Do it again" to the moon. . . . It may be that He has the eternal appetite of infancy; for we have sinned and grown old, and our Father is younger than we.[1]

The only reason things seem monotonous to us is because we live in bodies that grow tired, but in heaven we will have none of those limitations. We will be like children saying to the Father, "Do it again, Dad!"

Why do people who have many entertainment options tend to get bored easily?

Do you think you will ever get bored of being in the presence of God? Why or why not?

Heavenly Father, I can't imagine what it will be like to be with You forever, in a body that never grows old or tired. Fill me with anticipation for the day when I can say for eternity, "Do it again!"

Heaven Is a Place
of Indescribable Worship

> I heard the voice of many angels around the throne
> and the living creatures and the elders . . . saying
> with a loud voice, "Worthy is the Lamb that was
> slain to receive power and riches and wisdom and
> might and honor and glory and blessing."
> —Revelation 5:11–12

Some people believe the myth that heaven is an unending church service. Let's be honest: the idea of heaven being one long church service is a yawn fest. But the reason we feel that way is we don't understand what worship will be like in heaven. In heaven, we are going to be worshiping God as we have never worshiped Him before.

Think about a worship experience when you were moved to the innermost parts of your being and felt deeply connected to God. Think about that great moment of worship and multiply it by a million. That is what heaven is going to be like, because in heaven we will actually see Jesus face-to-face. No experience will match that. In Revelation 5:11–12, John described the worship we will experience in heaven: "I heard the voice of many angels around the throne and the living creatures and the elders; and the number of them was myriads of myriads, and thousands

In heaven, we are going to be worshiping God as we have never worshiped Him before.

of thousands, saying with a loud voice, 'Worthy is the Lamb that was slain to receive power and riches and wisdom and might and honor and glory and blessing.'" They praised with a loud voice.

On December 2, 2013, fans of the Seattle Seahawks set a world record as the loudest fans in the NFL. During a third-down defensive stand against the New Orleans Saints, the Seahawks fans produced an ear-splitting 137.6 decibels. (The roar of a jet engine one hundred feet away produces 140 decibels.) The Seahawks fans' "praise" was so loud it triggered a minor earthquake! Now that is the kind of worship we are going to have in heaven. The prophet Isaiah said, "The foundations of the thresholds trembled at the voice of him who called out [in worship]" (6:4). In heaven, we are going to have loud, exuberant worship.

Quiet moments of reflection are great for your personal worship with God, but in the Bible when God's people get together, they are never quiet. No, it is a time of celebration and praise, and that is what it is going to be like in heaven. Heaven is going to be a time of large worship, with tens of millions of people worshiping.

How does the worship described in Revelation 5 compare to the worship in your church?

What do you think it will be like to worship God in heaven?

Lord Jesus, You are worthy to be worshiped and praised! Show me ways that I can worship You today as I look forward to praising You in heaven for all eternity.

Worship in Heaven

Whether, then, you eat or drink or whatever you
do, do all to the glory of God.

—1 Corinthians 10:31

When we get to heaven, we are going to participate in inde-scribable worship, but is that all we are going to do? Is heaven only going to be a time of unending worship? The answer to that question is yes and no. It depends on how you define *worship*. If you define *worship* as a formal time of God's people getting together to praise God, then no, that is not all we are going to do in heaven. But in the Bible, worship is more than just formal times when we assemble together.

In 1 Corinthians 10:31, Paul said, "Whether, then, you eat or drink or whatever you do, do all to the glory of God." There is a way of going through the day—conducting your work,

We will worship God continually in heaven just as we should be doing here on earth.

sitting down for a meal, or relaxing—where God is always a part of your existence, and that is what worship is in the broader sense.

Worship is the continual awareness of, gratitude toward, and submission to God in everything we do. And in that sense, we will worship God continually in heaven just as we should be doing here on earth.

While worshiping God will be a central activity in heaven, it will not be our only activity. Just as Christians today can offer praise to God while engaging in other tasks throughout the week, Christians in the new heaven and new earth will worship God during special, designated times as well as while involved in other activities.

———————

How would you define *worship*?

What are some specific ways you can worship God today as you go about your daily routine?

> *God, help me to be continually aware of You, to be grateful for Your many blessings, and to submit to You in everything I do. May I worship You today in all my thoughts, words, and actions.*

Heaven Is a Place of Enjoyable Work

> My Father is working until now, and I Myself am working.
>
> —John 5:17

Heaven will not only be a time of indescribable worship but will also be a place of enjoyable work. Before you rebel at the idea of working in heaven, remember that God is a worker. God did not just create the universe in six days and then go into retirement. He took one day off, but that is all He took off. In John 5:17, Jesus said this about God: "My Father is working until now, and I Myself am working." God is a worker.

You and I were created in the image of God, and therefore we, too, were created to be workers. Although Eden was perfect, it was not self-sustaining. God did His part in creating this slice of Paradise on earth, but He gave people the responsibility of cultivating it—tilling the soil and planting and harvesting crops. In Genesis 2:15, God gave this assignment to Adam: "Then the LORD God took the man and put him into the garden of Eden to cultivate it and keep it."

You and I were created in the image of God, and therefore we, too, were created to be workers.

Many people believe that work is a curse from God, that it was a punishment for humankind's sin against God. That is not true. Genesis 2:15 takes place before the fall in Genesis 3. In our original form, we were created to work. Now, it is true that after the sin of Genesis 3, work became harder for us, but work itself has never been a curse. It is a privilege God has given us because we are created in His image.

We all are to be involved in doing something productive. And it is going to be that way in heaven. If God wants us to be workers on earth, then He wants us to be workers in heaven as well.

———

Do you tend to view work as a curse or as a blessing?
How does sin affect our attitude toward and experience of work?

God, thank You for creating me in Your image and giving me the privilege of working, as You also work. Strengthen me to be productive in my job today, and give me Your perspective on my work.

Workers in Heaven

There will no longer be any curse.
—Revelation 22:3

If God wants us to be workers on earth, then He wants us to be workers in heaven as well. You may say, "Working for eternity? That sounds more like hell than heaven."

Think about your job right now. What is it that makes it unpleasant? Maybe it is because you get so tired. Or perhaps it is a strained relationship you have with a coworker or your boss. Or maybe it is the government regulations that just seem to keep piling up to make your work harder and harder and harder. Our work is hard because we live in a sin-infected world, but Revelation 22:3 says that in the new heaven and new earth the curse of sin will be removed. In heaven, we will be able to perform our work in bodies that never grow tired. We will have perfect relationships. We will not be overburdened with regulations, and we will not be fighting against an uncooperative environment. In heaven, we will experience the work that God intended for us to enjoy.

In heaven, we will experience the work that God intended for us to enjoy.

What will our work entail? First of all, our work will involve cultivating—that is, taking what God has created and making it even better. For example, cherries are good; cherry pie is very good. That is part of cultivating, improving upon what God has given us.

Second, our work will involve creating. As human beings, we have been given the ability to create something out of nothing. For example, in the garden of Eden, Adam used his creativity to name the animals. Today we see our God-given creativity at work in the invention of the automobile, the airplane, and the smartphone. In heaven, we will use the gifts God has given us. Some people may write books, other people may produce music, and other people may produce movies. There is no telling how God will use our creativity in heaven.

What is your dream job?
What do you think your work will be like in heaven?

Lord, thank You for giving us the privilege and responsibility of cultivating Your creation. Whenever I struggle with frustrations in my job on earth, help me to look forward to the perfect work You will provide for me in heaven.

Ruling and Reigning with God

They will reign forever and ever.
—Revelation 22:5

Some people are created to rule over God's creation. That was God's plan for Adam and Eve.

> Then God said, "Let Us make man in Our image, according to Our likeness; and let them rule over the fish of the sea and over the birds of the sky and over the cattle and over all the earth, and over every creeping thing that creeps on the earth." (Gen. 1:26)

Adam and Eve were created to be coregents with God on earth. Because of sin they had to abdicate their rule, but in the new heaven and new earth, you and I will be corulers with God. Revelation 22:5 says we will "reign forever and ever."

Obviously, not everybody is going to be reigning, or there would be nobody to reign over. So who will be reigning with God?

Those who rule and reign with Christ need to have the desire to rule. For some people, the idea of being in charge makes you break out in a cold sweat. Don't worry. If you do not enjoy ruling, you are not going to be ruling in heaven. There has to be a desire. Second, you need to be able to rule. Romans 12 says one of the spiritual gifts is leadership. Third—and this is

Some people are created to rule over God's creation.

important—faithfulness is a criterion for leadership in God's kingdom. You can have the desire and even the ability to rule, but you also have to have a track record of faithfulness to God.

The single greatest determiner of leadership responsibilities in the next life will be faithfulness to God in this life. In Luke 19, Jesus told the parable of the minas to show that how we handle the time, treasures, and opportunities God has given us here on earth will determine what responsibility we have in eternity.

In what ways are you demonstrating faithfulness to God in this life? What specific things can you begin to do today to be more faithful with your time, treasures, and opportunities?

God, it is humbling to realize that in the new heaven and new earth, You will entrust us to rule and reign. May I be diligent today to develop a track record of faithfulness to You.

Christians Will Judge the World

If we endure, we will also reign with Him.
—2 Timothy 2:12

Besides worshiping God and working in heaven, some people will also be ruling and reigning with God.

What does reigning involve? There are two aspects of ruling with Christ. The first aspect of ruling is judging. In the first century, the people in the church at Corinth were fussing and fighting with one another; they could not come to an agreement. Paul said it should not be this way. He explained in 1 Corinthians 6:2, "Do you not know that the saints will judge the world?" One day, Christians will judge the world. That word *judge* means "to render a verdict."

While there is no evidence that you and I will be judging other people in the new heaven and new earth, the Bible is clear that we are going to judge angels. Paul continued in verse 3, "Do you not know that we will judge angels?" Perhaps he was referring to the fallen angels who are awaiting judgment for their sin described in Genesis 6. Or Paul may have used "judge" as a synonym for our responsibility of ruling over the angelic orders in the new heaven and new earth. We will have to wait for heaven to find the answer to this question.

The second aspect of ruling is governing. I believe that those who rule with Christ during the millennium and in the new heaven and new earth will be primarily involved in governing Christians who will work in Christ's glorious new kingdom. In 2 Timothy 2:12, Paul said, "If we endure, we will also reign with Him." In the Old Testament, we see examples of God's people reigning over certain territory. Joseph was prime minister over Egypt, Daniel over Babylon, and Mordecai over Persia. In heaven, we are going to be ruling over parts of God's creation.

In heaven, we are going to be ruling over parts of God's creation.

Although Scripture provides few details about what ruling in God's new kingdom will entail, we can be confident that the experience will be exhilarating and eternally fulfilling, since it is a reward for faithfulness to God in this life.

What do you think it will be like to rule and reign over God's new kingdom?

Why does God consider our faithfulness to Him in this life in determining our heavenly rewards?

God, I want to be faithful on earth as I prepare for my eternal life in Your new kingdom. Help me use my time, talents, and treasures today to further Your kingdom rather than my own.

Permanent Perks of Heaven

> Many will come from east and west, and recline at the table with Abraham, Isaac and Jacob in the kingdom of heaven.
>
> —Matthew 8:11

In heaven, we will have work to do, but we are not going to work all the time. We are also going to have some fun in heaven!

Heaven will be a time of enjoying other believers. God made us in such a way that we need fellowship with other human beings, and in heaven we are going to enjoy that in a way we never experienced on earth. In heaven, gone will be the impure motives, suspicions, and sins that taint relationships today.

We are also going to have some fun in heaven!

Think about how fascinating it is going to be to talk with your great-great-grandparents who are in heaven and learn more about your family. Or think what it will be like to hear Noah tell about what it was like on that ark, or David describe his miraculous victory over Goliath, or the disciples describe the first Easter morning. Think about talking theology with Martin Luther or science with Blaise Pascal. Think about talking to courageous leaders like William Wilberforce, or those who wrote beloved hymns like Fanny Crosby. Can you imagine sitting down and having a book review with C. S. Lewis or Flannery O'Connor?

From our first day in heaven, and for every day thereafter, we will walk the streets of the new heaven and new earth with astonishment: "There goes Jeremiah! And over there is Eve. I can't believe it—there's Paul talking with John and Charles Wesley. And over there is Esther . . . and Caleb . . . and John . . . and Solomon . . . and . . ."

That is what we are going to be doing in heaven—enjoying perfect fellowship with one another.

———

Who are some people you hope to meet or reunite with in heaven? What questions will you ask them?

> *God, I look forward to the fellowship I will experience with other believers in heaven! Thank You for preparing a place where I can develop relationships free from struggle, suspicions, and sin.*

Learning More about God in Heaven

The earth will be filled with the knowledge of the glory of the LORD.

—Habakkuk 2:14

Heaven will be a time of learning more about God. The prophet Habakkuk promised that "the earth will be filled with the knowledge of the glory of the LORD" (2:14). But have you ever wondered how that knowledge will come? When we die, is there a sudden information dump into our brains where we know everything about God? Maybe. But think about your most important relationships on earth. Hasn't part of the enjoyment of that relationship been learning more about that person over a period of time rather than learning everything at once? There is joy in discovery. I have spent fifty years getting to know my wife, Amy. I still have a lot more to discover, and the process has been exhilarating. It will be the same way in our relationship with God. I think we will have all eternity to get to know Him.

God has a great, indescribable future planned for those who love Him.

Heaven will also be a time of experiencing real rest. In heaven, we will be engaged in meaningful work, but that does not mean that is all we are going to do. With the Israelites, God set aside a day of rest every week. He also set aside certain weeks and certain months, and sometimes there was a year of rest as well. I think we will experience the same thing in heaven. There will be times we will rest from our labors, times we will be able to have true satisfaction in a job well done. That rest reminds us that as important as our work is here and will be in heaven, there is more to life than working.

Heaven will be a place of enjoying the perfect fellowship with others and perfect relationship with God we have always longed for. That is what we will be doing in heaven. Aren't you ready to go? God has a great, indescribable future planned for those who love Him.

———

When is the last time you were able to rest from your labor?

Why do you think God designed heaven as a place where we can experience genuine rest?

Heavenly Father, thank You for giving me the opportunity to learn more about You for all eternity. May I continually seek to know You in this life as I look forward to the wonderful future You have planned for me in heaven.

Traveling to the Wrong Destination

> Not everyone who says to Me, "Lord, Lord," will
> enter the kingdom of heaven, but he who does the
> will of My Father who is in heaven will enter.
> —Matthew 7:21

Maps can be very useful when you are traveling in unfamiliar territory. I discovered that truth the hard way a number of years ago.

A pastor friend invited me to speak at his church in Canada. So I got on a plane in Dallas and traveled to Winnipeg, Manitoba. I arrived about four o'clock in the afternoon, retrieved my luggage, walked outside the terminal, and waited for the pastor to pick me up. I waited, and I waited. No pastor. So I retrieved his letter of invitation, and I noticed that the address in the return portion of the letter did not match where I was. I had spoken for him before in Winnipeg, and I had assumed he was still in Winnipeg. Realizing I had a problem, I went to the airline ticket counter and said, "This letter says I'm supposed to be in Vancouver, British Columbia. Is there a bus I can catch? I need to be there in about thirty minutes." They laughed and said, "Vancouver is fifteen hundred miles from here."

"Oh no!" I said. "What am I going to do?" They said, "We have a plane that is getting ready to leave for Vancouver. Since you gain two hours going west, if you get on that plane right now, you can make it there in an hour Vancouver's time. We'll hold the plane for you." I ran to the gate, gave the agent my boarding pass, and was about to go down the jetway when the agent stopped me and gave me a map of Canada. He said, "Read this. It will help you the next time you come to our country."

Traveling to the wrong location can be embarrassing. But there is one time in your life you do not want to end up at the wrong destination, and that is the day of your death.

One of the greatest surprises about heaven is who is going to be there.

One of the greatest surprises about heaven is who is going to be there. When that day comes, we are going to be surprised to find that many of the people we thought were going to be there will not be in heaven. And we will be surprised that many people we thought would never be there will end up in heaven.

Have you ever gotten lost?

What could you have done differently to avoid that situation?

How often do you use maps in your everyday life?

God, thank You for providing a clear "road map" to heaven in Your Word. Help me to make sure I am on that road by placing my faith in Jesus Christ to forgive my sins and provide the way for me to spend eternity with You.

Who Will Be in Heaven?

The word of God is . . . able to judge the thoughts
and intentions of the heart.

—Hebrews 4:12

Sometimes when I am debating people on TV, they will say,
"Only God can decide who is going to be in heaven." That is
absolutely true. Only God can decide who will be in heaven.
The fact is, He has already decided that, and He has made His
decision public. He said there is only one way to heaven, and
that is through faith in Jesus Christ.

The Bible clearly says that only those who have trusted in
Christ for the forgiveness of their sins will reside in the new
heaven and new earth. When we declare that faith in Christ
offers the only path to heaven, we are not creating our own
criterion but simply repeating the requirement God established. The popular belief that all religions in the world lead
to God negates the most basic teaching of Jesus, who declared,
"I am the way, and the truth, and the life; no one comes to
the Father but through Me" (John 14:6). The God who never
changes is not going to surprise us by saying at the last minute,
"I've changed My mind about this 'faith in Jesus' requirement.
Everyone's welcome—come on in!"

Since only God is "able to judge the thoughts and intentions
of the heart" (Heb. 4:12), He alone knows who has sincerely
placed his or her faith in Christ for the forgiveness of sins. I
think we will be surprised to find that many people we thought

would have never trusted in Christ actually did end up trusting in Christ as Savior. But we are also going to be surprised that many people we thought did trust in Christ had, in fact, never trusted in Christ for salvation in their hearts. Hopefully you won't be surprised about your *own* eternal fate. If you wait until you have passed from this life into the next life to see whether you are welcomed into God's presence, you will have waited too long.

> *The Bible indicates many people will be surprised by their eternal destination.*

The Bible indicates many people will be surprised by their eternal destination. It will be the surprise of a lifetime when they discover that although they thought they were going to be welcomed into heaven, God turns them away.

Why do you think so many people believe that all religions in the world lead to God?

How does that belief compare to the teachings of Jesus Christ?

Jesus, thank You for telling us clearly that You are the way, the truth, and the life, and only by placing their faith in You will people be welcomed into heaven. Give me the courage to share the good news of Your salvation with those around me today.

The Worst Surprise of All

> Many will say to Me on that day, "Lord, Lord, did we not prophesy in Your name, and in Your name cast out demons, and in Your name perform many miracles?" And then I will declare to them, "I never knew you; depart from Me, you who practice lawlessness."
> —Matthew 7:22–23

Many people sincerely believe they are going to heaven. They sincerely follow other supposed paths that lead to heaven, such as Hinduism, Islam, and Buddhism. But it does not matter how sincere you are; you can be sincerely wrong.

How can you know if you are on the road to heaven? In Matthew 7:21–23, Jesus said,

> Not everyone who says to Me, "Lord, Lord," will enter the kingdom of heaven, but he who does the will of My Father who is in heaven will enter. Many will say to Me on that day, "Lord, Lord, did we not prophesy in Your name, and in Your name cast out demons, and in Your name perform many miracles?" And then I will declare to them, "I never knew you; depart from Me, you who practice lawlessness."

What day was Jesus talking about? He was talking about judgment day. He said that on that day, not just a few people are going to be surprised—many people who thought God would welcome them into heaven are going to be turned away. Why is that? Simple: they were on the wrong road the whole time.

The Bible teaches that there are two roads in life that lead to two very different destinations. Jesus explained in Matthew 7:13–14 that there are two roads that lead to two destinations. He said,

> *The Bible teaches that there are two roads in life that lead to two very different destinations.*

Enter through the narrow gate; for the gate is wide and the way is broad that leads to destruction, and there are many who enter through it. For the gate is small and the way is narrow that leads to life, and there are few who find it.

There are two roads in life. One is a broad road. It is the highway that leads, ultimately, to hell. Jesus said most people are on that road. But Jesus said there is another road going in the opposite direction that is very narrow. It leads to heaven, and very few people are on that road.

Do you know people who sincerely believe they can get to heaven by good works or some other religion?

What Bible verses could you share with them about the road to heaven?

Lord, thank You that while culture and popular opinion may change, Your Word never changes. The road to heaven may be narrow, but You have clearly described the path. Give me opportunities to share the gospel with those who are on the wrong road.

We Have a Sin Problem

All have sinned and fall short of the glory of God.
—Romans 3:23

No one accidentally ends up in heaven or hell without warning. Instead, there are four definite "signposts" along the way, alerting us as to whether or not we are on the right path leading to the right destination. The journey to heaven (or hell) begins in this life. If we are truly on the road that leads to heaven, then there are signposts we must acknowledge along the way.

Signpost #1 is: We have a sin problem. When most people see this signpost, they refuse to go any further. They say, "I do not like being called a sinner. That is insulting to me." So when they see that sign, they say, "I am getting on a different road."

But the fact is, God says we are all sinners. Romans 3:10–12 says, "There is none righteous, not even one; there is none who understands, there is none who seeks for God; all have turned aside, together they have become useless; there is none who does good, there is not even one." And then the climax is verse 23, "All have sinned and fall short of the glory of God." How many good people are there in the world? How many people are righteous? The word *righteous* in verse 10 means "in a right standing with God." Whom does God look at and say, "That is a really good person"? None. No one is righteous according to God's

The fact is, God says we are all sinners.

perfect standard. Some have sinned more than others, but we have all sinned and fallen short of God's plan for our lives.

Paul went on to say in Romans 6:23, "For the wages of sin is death." The payment for sin is not just physical death but spiritual death. That word *death* in Greek means "separation." Just as physical death is the separation of the body from the spirit, eternal death is the separation of the spirit from God. We all deserve that sentence, because we have all sinned before God. We inherited a virus called sin, and the Bible says because of that we are all guilty before God.

Why do people tend to think that only really bad people are sinners? According to the Bible, which people are sinners? What is the consequence of sin?

God, I confess that I am a sinner, and I know I deserve eternal separation from You. Thank You for sending Your Son, Jesus, to pay the penalty of my sin and provide salvation for me.

God Is Sinless

You shall be holy, for I am holy.
—1 Peter 1:16

We are looking at four signposts that represent essential truths you must acknowledge if you are on the road to heaven. Signpost #1 is: We have a sin problem. All of us are sinners, and we all deserve the punishment of eternal separation from God.

Signpost #2 is: God is sinless. No fewer than six times in the Bible, God said, "Be holy, for I am holy." That word *holy* means "different, separate, above." God is different than we are. We are sinful. God is sinless. Many people do not understand that. They say, "Why is God so judgmental about sin? Why can't God be more like me? I find it easy to overlook the faults of other people, and I can overlook my own faults. Why can't God be as tolerant as I am?"

The fact that you and I can overlook sin is not because we are so like God; it is because we are so unlike God. We tolerate sin because we are sinful. But God is not like we are. Habakkuk 1:13 says about God, "Your eyes are too pure to approve evil, and You can not look on wickedness with favor." God has zero tolerance for sin because He is holy.

God has zero tolerance for sin because He is holy.

When you couple this truth (God is sinless) with the first signpost (we have a sin problem), you can get discouraged pretty easily. For example, imagine you are on a road trip from

Oklahoma to Winnipeg, and you see a sign that says, "Winnipeg 1,000 miles." It's a long trip, but with perseverance you can make it—until you notice you have only a quarter of a tank of gas left. You pull into a gas station, only to realize you have no wallet. A quarter of a tank of gas is not enough to get to Winnipeg. All you can do is make a U-turn and try to make it home.

The same is true for us. On our journey to heaven, none of us has enough spiritual gas, or goodness, to get into heaven. Now, some people have a quarter of a tank, some people might have half a tank, some people might have seven-eighths of a tank full of goodness in their own lives. But none of us has enough righteousness to get to heaven. That is why Romans 3:23 says, "All have sinned and fall short of the glory of God."

What do you think it means for God to be holy?

Why does God have zero tolerance for sin?

God, I praise You for Your absolute holiness. You are perfect and pure in every way, and You cannot tolerate sin. Thank You for sending Jesus to cover my sin with His perfect sacrifice.

Our Need for a Savior

> As many as received Him, to them He gave the right to become children of God, even to those who believe in His name.
>
> —John 1:12

There are four signposts that represent four truths we must acknowledge if we are to be on the road to heaven. Signpost #1 is: We have a sin problem. We are all guilty before God. Signpost #2 is: God is sinless. He has zero tolerance for sin. What are the remaining signposts?

Signpost #3 is: Jesus is the solution to our sin problem. Imagine you are on a road trip and do not have enough gas to get where you are going. Suddenly, a big tanker stops, and

Jesus is the solution to our sin problem.

the driver says, "This is your lucky day. I have all the gas you can possibly use, and I am willing to let you have some of it. May I fill your tank for you?"

That is exactly what Jesus does for us. When Jesus died on the cross, two amazing transactions took place. First, Jesus took the punishment we deserve for our sins. God is holy and cannot overlook evil. Nahum 1:3 says, "The LORD will by no means leave the guilty unpunished." Someone has to pay for our sins—and Jesus volunteered to do just that. When Jesus died on the cross, in some inexplicable way He took all the punishment from God that you and I deserve.

Second, Jesus gave us His goodness, which we also do not deserve. That is why 2 Corinthians 5:21 says, "[God] made [Jesus] who knew no sin to be sin on our behalf, so that we might become the righteousness of God in Him." Because Jesus is the sinless Son of God, He alone can give us the righteousness we do not deserve. Romans 5:1 says, "Having been justified by faith, we have peace with God through our Lord Jesus Christ."

The signpost declaring Jesus to be the only solution to bridge the gap between our sinfulness and God's holiness causes many people to stumble and search for an alternate road to heaven. We must either embrace Jesus's claim that He is God's Son or reject it. There is no intellectually honest alternative. Jesus said, "I am the way, and the truth, and the life; no one comes to the Father but through Me" (John 14:6).

Because of the two transactions that took place on the cross—Jesus Christ receiving the punishment we deserve and our receiving the righteousness we don't deserve—God offers us entrance into heaven.

What qualifies Jesus to be the only one who could pay the price for our sin?

Why do you think so many people reject Jesus and search instead for alternate ways to heaven?

Jesus, thank You for dying on the cross to take the punishment I deserve and giving me Your righteousness, which I don't deserve. I am forever grateful for Your sacrifice, which enables me to have eternal peace with God.

Choose to Accept Christ's Forgiveness

> As many as received Him, to them He gave the right to become children of God, even to those who believe in His name.
>
> —John 1:12

When most people hear that they are guilty before God and deserve His punishment, they go the opposite direction. Others are willing to admit their mistakes but can't come to grips with the idea that Jesus Christ is the only solution to our need for God's forgiveness, so they start looking for a different spiritual path.

However, there are some people who agree that they are sinners deserving punishment, that God is holy and demands complete perfection, and that Jesus is the only solution to their need for God's forgiveness. Yet their response is just to stop where they are and not take the final step to embrace the last signpost on the highway to heaven.

Signpost #4 is: We must choose to accept Christ's offer of forgiveness.

Once again, imagine you are on a road trip but do not have enough gas to make it where you are going. Next to you is a gas tanker, and the driver has offered to put gas in your car. There has to be a point when you unscrew your gas cap and allow that

We must choose to accept Christ's offer of forgiveness.

tanker to fill your empty tank. And it is the same way in our relationship with God. You can believe that you are a sinner and that God is holy. You can believe that Jesus paid the price for your sins. But there has to be a time when God transfers the righteousness of His Son into your life so that when God looks at you, He no longer sees your sin; He sees the righteousness of His Son, Jesus Christ. John 1:12 says it this way: "As many as received Him, to them He gave the right to become children of God, even to those who believe in His name."

We all have varying amounts of goodness in our spiritual gas tank. Some people have half a tank, some people have a quarter of a tank, and some are bone-dry. None of us has enough, but God offers His forgiveness to everyone who asks. It does not matter what you have done—God is able and willing to forgive you and to welcome you into heaven if you are willing to ask. Romans 10:13 says, "Whoever will call on the name of the Lord will be saved."

Why is simply knowing about Jesus not enough for salvation? According to the Bible, what must we do to receive Christ's offer of forgiveness?

> *God, thank You for being able and willing to forgive me and welcome me into heaven when I trust in Jesus Christ and ask for Your forgiveness. I praise You for offering Your forgiveness to everyone who is willing to ask.*

Do People in Heaven Know What Is Happening on Earth?

> Since we have so great a cloud of witnesses surrounding us . . . let us run with endurance the race that is set before us.
>
> —Hebrews 12:1

Do people in heaven know what is happening on earth? A lot of people wonder about that. The answer is absolutely. People in heaven know what is happening on earth and under the earth. Let's look at Scripture passages that give us some insight on that subject.

Hebrews 12:1 is often used to say people in heaven are aware of what is happening on earth. The verse reads, "Since we have so great a cloud of witnesses surrounding us . . . let us run with endurance the race that is set before us." Who is this "cloud of witnesses surrounding us"? Remember, there are no chapter divisions in the original text. This phrase refers back to chapter 11: Abraham, Isaac, Jacob, Noah, Rahab, and all the other men and women of faith are this cloud of witnesses. And right now, the Bible says, they are in heaven, surrounding us.

People in heaven know what is happening on earth and under the earth.

Some people think that since these witnesses are surrounding us, they are like fans in the bleachers watching us as we live our lives. But that can be disconcerting. Do you really want

108

to think of Solomon, who wrote a book on the intimacies of marital love, peeping into your bedroom and critiquing what is going on? I don't think so. Do you really want to think of your grandmother or your great-grandmother in heaven watching every move you make? That is kind of disturbing, isn't it?

Is that what Hebrews 12:1 is teaching? I don't think so. I think this passage really does not say people in heaven can tell what is happening on earth. In the context, the "cloud of witnesses" refers only to those Old Testament saints mentioned in Hebrews 11. The point the writer of Hebrews is making is that in light of the example of those who persevered in their faith, we should also keep moving forward in obeying God regardless of the obstacles we face. What the writer was simply saying was this: "Consider these great men and women and the way they lived their lives. We ought to demonstrate the same kind of faith in following their example."

Think of someone you consider to be a hero of the Christian faith. What can you do today to follow his or her example of faithfulness to God?

God, thank You for the legacy of men and women who served You obediently and well. Help me live today in a way that follows their example of faithfulness to You.

People in Heaven Are Immediately Aware

> We have become a spectacle to the world, both to angels and to men.
>
> —1 Corinthians 4:9

There are some passages in the Bible that indicate people in heaven do know what is happening on earth. For example, Christ must be aware of the obedience and disobedience of Christians on earth since He condemned and commended the seven churches in Revelation 2–3. Furthermore, the apostle Paul realized that a heavenly audience was witnessing his actions on earth since he described his life as "a spectacle to the world, both to angels and to men" (1 Cor. 4:9). We can assume from this verse that angels are also aware of the activities of people on earth.

Also, consider the story of Lazarus and the rich man that Jesus told in Luke 16. In this story, there were two men who lived two very different lives: a rich man and a poor man named Lazarus. The Bible says when they both died, Lazarus went directly to heaven, to Abraham's bosom, because he had placed his faith in God. However, the rich man immediately ended up in hades, the temporary residence of the unsaved dead. By the way, this story dispels the belief that a soul sleeps for a long period of time when a person dies. Jesus said the rich man instantly knew he was in hades, and he saw that Lazarus was in Abraham's bosom. Luke 16:23 says, "In Hades [the rich

110

man] lifted up his eyes, being in torment, and saw Abraham far away and Lazarus in his bosom."

Both the rich man and Lazarus were conscious of what was happening in the other's world. Notice that Abraham knew of the suffering of the rich man in hades, and the rich man in hades was aware of the comfort Lazarus was being offered in heaven.

> *People in heaven know what is happening in hell, and people in hell know what is happening in heaven.*

It appears that people in heaven know what is happening in hell, and people in hell know what is happening in heaven.

Have you ever heard someone say that death is like being asleep or simply ceasing to exist?

How does Jesus's story in Luke 16 clarify what we experience beyond the grave?

God, thank You for Your Word, which gives us the truth about life beyond this world. Help me today to bring glory to You, knowing that my life is "a spectacle to the world, both to angels and to men."

People in Heaven Are Aware of Events on Earth

> Hallelujah! Salvation and glory and power belong to our God; because His judgments are true and righteous; for He has judged the great harlot who was corrupting the earth with her immorality, and He has avenged the blood of His bond-servants on her.
> —Revelation 19:1–2

Do people in heaven know what is happening on earth? The answer is yes.

In Revelation 6, we see the tribulation martyrs and the judgment on earth. At the rapture of the church, all Christians who are living on earth at that time will be taken to be with the Lord. Only unbelievers will be left on the earth for the final seven years of earth's history. During those seven years of tribulation, some people will be saved—but just as many Christians around the world today are being slaughtered today for their faith, these future "tribulation saints" will pay a steep price for their salvation. They will have to give their lives as martyrs.

John described what he saw in heaven during the tribulation: "I saw underneath the altar the souls of those who had been slain because of the word of God, and because of the testimony which they had maintained" (Rev. 6:9). These are Christians who were slain during the tribulation. John saw them in heaven. "They cried out with a loud voice, saying, 'How long, O Lord, holy and true, will You refrain from judging and avenging our blood on those who dwell on the earth?'" (v. 10). These tribulation saints looked down from heaven and saw that those who had killed them were still running unchecked throughout the world. So they were saying, "God, how long are You going to allow this to continue? When are You going to bring judgment against those who rebel against You?" Now, they could not say that unless they were aware of what was happening on the earth.

They are aware of what is happening on the earth.

In Revelation 19:1–2, before the climactic battle of Armageddon, these saints in heaven say, "Hallelujah! Salvation and glory and power belong to our God; because His judgments are true and righteous; for He has judged the great harlot who was corrupting the earth with her immorality, and He has avenged the blood of His bond-servants on her." The tribulation saints in heaven are able to see God pouring out His judgment on Babylon—the world system opposed to God—because they are aware of what is happening on the earth.

Have you ever longed for God to judge evil?

What can you learn about God from the tribulation saints' response when they see God finally judging the evil world system?

> *Lord, You hold the future in Your perfect, sovereign hands. Thank You for Your assurance that someday You will judge this evil world and create a perfect new heaven and new earth.*

Saints in Heaven Rejoice When Sinners Repent

> There is joy in the presence of the angels of God over one sinner who repents.
>
> —Luke 15:10

Jesus loved to tell stories. Three of His most famous stories are in Luke 15: the parables of the lost sheep, the lost coin, and the lost son. All three of these stories had the same purpose: to contrast the attitude of the self-righteous Pharisees, who hated sinners, with the attitude of the truly righteous God, who *loves* sinners. Jesus's point in all three parables was the same: when you lose something of value—a sheep, a coin, a child—you don't hate the lost object. Instead, you search for it diligently and rejoice when you find it.

Jesus was saying that God has the same attitude toward people who are living apart from Him. God doesn't hate lost people. He loves them, He searches for them, and He rejoices when He is reunited with them. Jesus said in Luke 15:10, "There is joy in the presence of the angels of God over one sinner who repents."

Who rejoices in heaven when the unsaved are saved? We know God rejoices. And I have always heard that the angels rejoice, but that is not what this verse says. It does not say the angels rejoice—though they probably do. Jesus said, "There is joy *in the presence* of the angels of God" when a sinner

114

repents. Who is rejoicing in the presence of angels? It is the residents of heaven.

Christians in heaven are celebrating the salvation of sinners on earth. Think about this: besides God, who in heaven would appreciate the salvation of a non-Christian (especially if that non-Christian happened to be a friend or family member) more than those who had already experienced redemption?

The saints in heaven rejoice when they see a sinner on earth repent. If citizens of heaven rejoice at the salvation of sinners, then they not only know what is taking place on earth in a general sense but are aware of the specific choices individuals are making on earth. Yes, people in heaven are aware of what happens on the earth.

> *Yes, people in heaven are aware of what happens on the earth.*

What is God's attitude toward lost people?

How does He respond when people repent?

How do you tend to respond when someone repents and comes to faith in Jesus Christ?

God, nothing is more joyful than when a lost person repents and trusts in You for salvation! May I rejoice with the saints in heaven when people put their faith in You.

Citizens of Heaven Are Aware of the Captives in Hell

> In Hades he lifted up his eyes, being in torment, and
> saw Abraham far away and Lazarus in his bosom.
> —Luke 16:23

Is it possible that people in heaven could see the horrors of hell? To answer that question, let's remind ourselves of why hell exists.

Hell was not a part of God's original creation. Hell was necessitated by the angels who joined Lucifer in his revolt against God, along with people who chose to rebel against God. Warren Wiersbe explained the necessity of hell this way:

> Hell is a witness to the righteous character of God. He must judge sin. Hell is also a witness to man's responsibility, the fact that man is not a robot or a helpless victim, but a creature able to make choices. God does not "send people to hell"; they send themselves by rejecting the Savior.[1]

Hell is a place to quarantine those who choose to separate themselves from God.

Hell is a place to quarantine those who choose to separate themselves from God.

The English word *hell* is a translation of three Greek words. The first word translated "hell" in the Bible is *hades*. Hades refers to the temporary place of the unsaved. When an unsaved person dies, he or she immediately goes to hades, as the rich man did in Luke 16:23. Hades is a place of physical suffering, but it is not the final place of the unsaved.

The second word translated "hell" in the Bible is *tartaros*. In 2 Peter 2:4, Peter wrote, "God did not spare angels when they sinned, but cast them into hell and committed them to pits of darkness, reserved for judgment." Peter was not talking about the angels who joined Lucifer in his revolt and were cast to earth; we call these demons. Demons are free to roam the earth and influence believers and unbelievers alike, except for the group of demons Peter described. These fallen angels committed a particularly heinous sin recorded in Genesis 6, and God confined them to a place of judgment.

The third word translated "hell" is *gehenna*, the lake of fire. Just as hades is the temporary location of the unsaved, gehenna is the final place of the unsaved. In Matthew 8:12, Jesus described gehenna as "the outer darkness," a place of "weeping and gnashing of teeth." Mark 9:48 says it is "where their worm does not die, and the fire is not quenched." This is the final destination of everyone who refuses to trust in Jesus Christ for the forgiveness of sins.

Why do you think people tend to avoid the subject of hell?
Why is hell a necessary place?

God, You are holy, and You must judge sin. Give me compassion for unbelievers and courage to share the gospel with them today so they might repent and trust in You.

What Is Hell Like?

If anyone's name was not found written in the book
of life, he was thrown into the lake of fire.

—Revelation 20:15

What is hell like? Just like heaven, hell is a physical location. The word *topos*, meaning geographical location, is used to describe heaven. Heaven is not a state of mind; it's a place. The same is true about hell. In the story of the rich man and Lazarus, hell is described as being "far away" and separated from heaven by a "great chasm" (Luke 16:23, 26).

There are three horrific descriptions of hell in the Bible. First of all, hell is a place of eternal physical torment. In Luke 16:24, the rich man cries out, "I am in agony in this flame." After the judgment of the unsaved, the residents of hell will be cast into the lake of fire (Rev. 20:15). Some theologians claim that people thrown into the lake of fire are instantly destroyed. This is the doctrine of annihilationism. But that's not what Scripture says. The Bible says the punishment of hell is eternal. In Revelation 20:10, after the final rebellion against God, "the devil who deceived them was thrown into the lake of fire and brimstone, where the beast and the false prophet are also; and they will be tormented day and night forever and ever." The word translated "forever and ever" is also used to describe the eternality of heaven. The same word that describes the eternality of heaven is used to describe the eternality of hell.

Second, the Bible teaches that hell is a place of indescribable loneliness. People think in hell they will party with all their friends. But Jesus said in Luke 13:28 that hell will be a place of "weeping and gnashing of teeth." Even if your friends are there, you will not know it because it is a place of complete darkness, according to Matthew 8:12. All you will be able to hear are the laments of those who are confined to that place of eternal punishment.

Hell is a place of no return.

Third, hell is a place of no return. That is perhaps the worst truth about hell: no one escapes. Again, in Jesus's story, Abraham says to the rich man, "Those who wish to come over from here [heaven] to you will not be able, and . . . none may cross over from there to us" (Luke 16:26). In hell, everybody will become a believer, but it will be too late. Hell is a place of no return.

Why do some people believe that hell is a big party with all their friends? How does the Bible describe hell?

Lord Jesus, someday every knee will bow and every tongue will confess that You are God. But by that time, it will be too late for those who did not place their faith in You on earth. Give me a sense of urgency today to share the good news of Your salvation.

Will Heaven's Joy Be Diminished by What Happens on Earth and in Hell?

> He comes to be glorified in His saints on that day,
> and to be marveled at among all who have believed.
> —2 Thessalonians 1:10

The Bible indicates that believers in heaven know what is taking place on earth, at least in some sense. And they know what is taking place in hell, according to the story of Lazarus and the rich man in Luke 16. So how can we be happy in heaven while watching those we care about on earth suffering from devastating illnesses, broken relationships, or destructive addictions?

And how could we ever enjoy one pleasure of the new heaven and new earth knowing that some of our friends and family members will be suffering in hell? How could you really enjoy all God had prepared for you—no matter how spectacular it was—knowing that your loved one was in hell and being tormented forever? How could that be heaven for anyone?

Some people have answered that question by saying, "God will purge our memories in heaven." People who believe that point to Isaiah 65:17, which says, "I create new heavens and a new earth; and the former things will not be remembered or come to mind." Yet in the context of that passage, God was talking about His mind, and the "former things" He was referring to are the former sins of Israel. In other words, in the new heaven and new earth, God will not remember the sins of His people. We find that throughout Scripture: whenever God forgives, He remembers our sins no more. That does not mean He develops a case of divine amnesia. It means He will not hold us accountable for our sins. When you forgive somebody, you make a choice not to hold their sin against them any longer. That is what God means when He says He will remember the former things no more.

> *We will remember the things on earth, and our relationships will continue in heaven.*

God does not do a memory wipe when we get to heaven. In fact, Scripture argues to the contrary. Our life is a continuum. We will remember the things on earth, and our relationships will continue in heaven.

Have you ever forgiven someone and decided not to hold the offense against him or her?

Why is it significant that when God forgives us, He chooses not to remember our sins?

> *God, thank You for forgiving my sins—and choosing not to remember them anymore! I look forward to the happy memories and relationships on earth that I will remember and continue in heaven.*

People in Heaven Understand the Plan and the Justice of God

He comes to be glorified in His saints on that day,
and to be marveled at among all who have believed.
—2 Thessalonians 1:10

Will the joy of heaven be diminished by what happens on earth and in hell?

Some people say, "We will be so caught up with the joys in heaven that we will not be aware of what is happening in hell." We see that phenomenon in our life every day. For example, there are millions of starving children in the world right now. But I bet that does not keep you from enjoying a meal today. Is it possible that when we get to heaven, we will be so preoccupied with the joys of heaven that we will not be aware of what is happening in hell?

Some people think the only reason we are able to enjoy life despite the suffering of others is that we are not like Jesus. But surely when we become like Jesus, we will weep over those in hell, right? Though Jesus wept over the unsaved when He was on earth, Scripture indicates He is experiencing unending joy in heaven. In fact, Hebrews 12:2 says Jesus endured the cross so He could experience "the joy set before Him." Jesus suffered on earth so He could experience joy in heaven, and the same is true for us. Psalm 16:11 describes what it will be like when we are in the presence of the Lord: "In Your presence is fullness of joy; in your right hand there are pleasures forever." In heaven, we will experience unending pleasure and joy.

In heaven, we will fully understand the plan and the justice of God. That is how we will handle the suffering in hell. When we see Jesus dealing out retribution to those who have not accepted the gospel, Christ the judge will "be marveled at among all who have believed" (2 Thess. 1:10). When we see Jesus in all of His glory, we will understand His ho-

> *Nothing that happens on earth or in hell will diminish in the slightest degree the unending joy God has planned for us in heaven.*

liness and His retribution against those who refuse to accept the gospel. Nothing that happens on earth or in hell will diminish in the slightest degree the unending joy God has planned for us in heaven.

Why should the hope of heaven fill us with joy?

What do you think it will be like to experience "fullness of joy" in heaven?

Lord, how wonderful it will be to experience unending pleasure and joy in heaven! I look forward to the day when I will see You in all Your glory and have "fullness of joy" in Your presence.

Will We Know One Another in Heaven?

Blessed and holy is the one who has a part in the first resurrection.

—Revelation 20:6

Growing old is not for the faint of heart. With age come aches, ailments, and sometimes a few extra pounds. Unfortunately, most people don't age gracefully. No, getting old reminds me a lot of what Jesus said to Peter in John 21:18: "I tell you the truth, when you were young you were able to do as you liked. You dressed yourself and went wherever you wanted to go, but when you are old, you will stretch out your hands, and others will dress you and take you where you don't want to go" (NLT). Can you identify with that? Part of growing older also means not always recognizing people. Have you ever had the experience of going to a high school or a college reunion? You see people but don't recognize them. If it wasn't for their nametag, you wouldn't know who they are. Even worse, they don't recognize you. And perhaps worst of all, have you ever stood in front of the mirror and looked at yourself and wondered, *Who is that person?*

This brings up an interesting question: When we get to heaven, what will our bodies be like? Will we know one another? Will other people know us? To find answers, we need to understand Jesus's promise of a resurrection body.

The Bible is very clear that in heaven, we are not going to be a bunch of spirits floating around. We are going to have physical bodies. That should not be a surprise when we remember that God's original design for us was both a spirit and a body. Genesis 2:7 says, "The LORD God formed man of dust from the ground, and breathed into his nostrils the breath of life; and man became a living being." God cre-

> *Believers' new bodies are necessary so that we can experience God's unending blessing.*

ated us as body and spirit, and in eternity we will always exist in body as well as spirit. God's future plan for us includes a physical resurrection.

It is not only Christians who will receive a new body; unbelievers will also receive a new body for eternity. Believers' new bodies are necessary so that we can experience God's unending blessing. Unbelievers must receive a body so that they can experience God's everlasting judgment. Everyone is going to be raised from the dead and have a resurrected body.

What do you wish you could change about your body?

How does it make you feel to know that you will receive a new body for eternity?

> *God, I praise You for uniquely designing me. Though in this world my body suffers the effects of sin, including aging and sickness, I look forward to the day when You will give me a new body to experience Your unending blessing.*

The Two Resurrections

Blessed and holy is the one who has a part in the
first resurrection; over these the second death has
no power.

—Revelation 20:6

The Bible talks about two resurrections. The resurrection for
Christians is called the first resurrection. In Revelation 20:6,
John says, "Blessed and holy is the one who has a part in the
first resurrection; over these the second death has no power."
The first resurrection doesn't refer to a point in time; it refers
to the people, believers, who will receive a new body to experience God's blessing.

Not every believer will receive his or her new body at the
same point in history. The apostle Paul made that clear in
1 Corinthians 15:22–23: "For as in Adam all die, so also in
Christ all will be made alive. But each in his own order." Some
of us will receive a resurrection body at the rapture. Other
believers will receive their new bodies at the second coming
of Jesus. And believers who are saved during the millennium
will receive their new bodies at the end of the thousand-year
reign of Christ. But all believers are part of the first resurrection, the resurrection of the saved.

The second resurrection is the resurrection of all the unsaved. One day, every unbeliever who has ever been born will
be raised from the dead. Right now, when unbelievers die, they
go to hades, the temporary place of the unsaved. But someday

they are going to be raised. Unlike the first resurrection, which occurs in stages, the second resurrection occurs at one point in history, before the great white throne judgment. It is described in Revelation 20:13: "The sea gave up the dead which were in it, and death and hades gave up the dead which were in them; and they were judged, every one of them according to their deeds." These unbelievers rejected the grace of God. And as good as their works may be, no one is good enough to inherit heaven. Verse 14 says, "Then death and hades were thrown into the lake of fire. This is the second death, the lake of fire." Everyone, believers and unbelievers, will receive a new body for all eternity.

> *Everyone, believers and unbelievers, will receive a new body for all eternity.*

What is the difference between the first resurrection and the second resurrection?

Why is it significant that, for Christians, "the second death has no power"?

God, thank You for Your gift of salvation, so that "in Christ all will be made alive." I look forward to the day when I will receive a new body to experience Your blessing in heaven forever.

The Analogy of Planting and Harvesting

> Flesh and blood cannot inherit the kingdom of God.
> —1 Corinthians 15:50

How can people who have died have bodies that come to life again? Think about a man whose body is donated to those who need the body parts. His eyes go to Ethel, his kidney goes to Sidney, and on and on until his body parts are distributed. How will God put all that together again? How is a resurrection possible?

The apostle Paul answered that question by using the analogy of planting and harvesting. In 1 Corinthians 15:36–38, he explained how a resurrection happens:

> That which you sow does not come to life unless it dies; and that which you sow, you do not sow the body which is to be, but a bare grain, perhaps of wheat or of something else. But God gives it a body just as He wished, and to each of the seeds a body of its own.

What is involved in planting and harvesting? First of all, when you plant a seed, the seed dies. If you plant a watermelon seed in the ground, that seed dies before it comes to life, and so it is with the resurrection. When we die, that death is necessary for there to be a future harvest.

Paul said death is not only inevitable but also necessary for us to inherit God's kingdom. In 1 Corinthians 15:36, he said, "That which you sow does not come to life unless it dies." He explained why in verse 50: "Flesh and blood cannot inherit the kingdom of God; nor does the perishable inherit the imperishable."

Death is not only inevitable but also necessary for us to inherit God's kingdom.

Think of it this way: your body is perfectly designed for this world, but your body is not suitable for residence on Mars. Your body is only suitable for this planet, and it is the same way in terms of this earth and the new heaven and new earth. That is why Paul said, "Flesh and blood cannot inherit the kingdom of God."

Why can't we go to heaven in our earthly bodies?

How does the analogy of planting and harvesting help you understand the need for your resurrection body?

Lord, You not only uniquely and perfectly designed my body for this world but also created a uniquely perfect body for me in the next world. Thank You for providing the resurrection body I need to inherit the kingdom of God.

Our Resurrection Bodies Are Superior Yet Similar

> It is sown a perishable body, it is raised an imper-
> ishable body; it is sown in dishonor, it is raised in
> glory; it is sown in weakness, it is raised in power.
> —1 Corinthians 15:42–43

In 1 Corinthians 15, the apostle Paul explained that when we die, our human bodies are like seeds that are planted in the ground. The death of our human bodies—regardless of how it occurs—is not a hindrance to a future resurrection but a pre-requisite for a greater harvest. It is necessary that our bodies be planted in the ground, so to speak, so that something better can be harvested later. We should not view death as the end of something great but as the beginning of something greater.

That leads to the second part of the process of resurrection, the reaping of the harvest. Notice something about the relationship between the planting and the harvest. First of all, the harvest is superior to the seed. For example, imagine it is a hot day, and you have been outside working in the yard. You come inside for some refreshment. You can either have a cold slice of watermelon, or you can eat a watermelon seed. Which would you choose? I think everybody would choose the slice of watermelon, because the harvest is always superior to the seed. It is the same way with the resurrection. What is harvested at the resurrection, our new body, is vastly superior to that which is planted. It is important to understand that we are not going to carry our old bodies into heaven. Aren't you grateful for that? Our old bodies are raised, but then they are completely renovated. And what we will receive from God is far superior to what was planted.

Second, the harvest is also similar to the seed. You don't plant a watermelon seed and harvest a kumquat. If you plant a watermelon seed, you get a watermelon, and it is the same way with us. When our bodies die, it is not someone else who is resurrected. We do not get a body that is totally dissimilar to what we were. Our new bodies are going to resemble our old bodies.

> *Our old bodies are raised, but then they are completely renovated.*

How could this understanding of death—not the end of something great but the beginning of something greater—give comfort and hope to people who are afraid of dying?

Lord, many things about my body are weary, aging, and broken. Thank You for Your promise that someday You will give me a completely renovated body that will be vastly superior to this one!

The Prototype of Our Resurrection Bodies Is Jesus

When He appears, we will be like Him, because we will see Him just as He is.

—1 John 3:2

If you want a good idea of what your resurrection body is going to be like for eternity, the best place to look is Jesus. Jesus is the prototype of our resurrection bodies. In 1 John 3:2, the apostle wrote, "We are children of God, and it has not appeared as yet what we will be. We know that when He appears, we will be like Him, because we will see Him just as He is."

If you want a good idea of what your resurrection body is going to be like for eternity, the best place to look is Jesus.

Was Jesus's resurrection spiritual or physical? Some people in the Corinthian church said, "We believe Jesus was raised from the dead, but we believe it was a spiritual resurrection." So Paul made it clear that the physical resurrection of Jesus is the very essence of the gospel. He wrote,

I delivered to you as of first importance what I also received, that Christ died for our sins according to the Scriptures, and that He was buried, and that He was raised on the third day according to the Scriptures. (1 Cor. 15:3–4)

The physical resurrection of Jesus is the heart of the gospel.

After Jesus was raised from the dead, He spent forty days ministering to people. On seventeen occasions, He conversed with His disciples. Three times, He ate with His disciples. On two occasions, He allowed His disciples to touch Him.

What was Jesus's resurrection body like? First, Jesus's resurrection body was superior to His earthly body. Jesus was without sin in His earthly body, but He had limitations just as you and I have in our earthly bodies. But in His resurrection body, Jesus was able to materialize in a place at will on several occasions, for example.

Second, Jesus's body was similar to His earthly body. During the forty days Jesus spent on earth after His resurrection, those who knew Him best eventually recognized Him. What caused them to recognize Jesus? There were some similarities between Jesus's earthly body and His new body. Perhaps it was His stature. Perhaps it was the color of His eyes or His hair. Perhaps it was a mannerism He had that caused the disciples to recognize Him. Whatever it was, Jesus's resurrection body clearly bore some resemblance to His earthly body.

Why is the physical resurrection of Jesus essential to the gospel?
In what ways do you think your resurrection body will be like Jesus's new body?

Lord Jesus, I believe that You died for my sins on the cross, were buried, and were raised on the third day. I look forward to the day when I will be like You, because I will see You as You are.

Our Resurrection Bodies Will Be Physical

> It is sown a perishable body, it is raised an imperishable body.
>
> —1 Corinthians 15:42

What will our resurrection bodies be like in heaven? Looking at Jesus, we can gather several important facts about our new bodies in heaven.

The Bible says that in heaven, our bodies will be physical.

The Bible says that in heaven, our bodies will be physical. Just as Jesus had a physical body after His resurrection, so will we. However, our new bodies will be vastly different from our earthly bodies. In 1 Corinthians 15:39–40, Paul said,

> All flesh is not the same flesh, but there is one flesh of men, and another flesh of beasts, and another flesh of birds, and another of fish. There are also heavenly bodies and earthly bodies, but the glory of the heavenly is one, and the glory of the earthly is another.

God designs our bodies just as He does animals, birds, fish, the stars, and the moon: all to serve their unique purpose. Paul continued,

> So also is the resurrection of the dead. It is sown a perishable body, it is raised an imperishable body; it is sown in dishonor,

it is raised in glory; it is sown in weakness, it is raised in power; it is sown a natural body, it is raised a spiritual body. (vv. 42–44)

The word *body* in this passage refers to a physical body. Repeating this word over and over was Paul's way of saying: "On earth, we have a natural body. In the new heaven and new earth, we will be spiritual, but we will still have a body."

———

What contrasts did Paul list in 1 Corinthians 15:42–44 between your earthly body and your resurrection body?

What do you look forward to most about your resurrection body?

Lord, sometimes I struggle in this earthly body that is weak and weary. Thank You for designing a new physical body for me that will be raised in glory and power!

Our Resurrection Bodies Will Be Perfect and Personal

See My hands and My feet, that it is I Myself.
—Luke 24:39

In heaven, our bodies will be perfect. No more cancer. No more heart attacks. No more strokes. No more high blood pressure. Revelation 21:4 says, "The first things have passed away." Revelation 22:3 says, "There will no longer be any curse."

Joni Eareckson Tada is a great woman of God who, through a diving accident at age seventeen, became a quadriplegic. Joni wrote this about the promise of a new body:

> Can you imagine the hope this gives to someone who has a spinal cord injury, like I do? Or someone who has cerebral palsy, a brain injury, or multiple sclerosis? Imagine the hope this gives someone who has bipolar disorder. No other religion, no other philosophy, promises new bodies, hearts, and minds. Only in the gospel of Christ do hurting people find such incredible hope.[1]

Isn't that great? That is the promise we have: in heaven, our bodies will be perfect.

In heaven, our bodies will also be personal. When we are raised from the dead, we do not become somebody else. We are still our individual selves. In 1 John 3:2, the apostle John said, "We will be like Him." That does not mean we all become mini-Jesuses without any distinction. It means we will inherit heavenly DNA like Jesus but will retain our own identities.

Think of it this way: when we upgrade computer software, we do not throw away the whole program; we upgrade it to a better state. And in the same way, when we are raised from the dead, it is a renovation, but we still are ourselves at the core. How do I know that? In Luke

In heaven, our bodies will be perfect.

24:39, when Jesus appeared to His disciples in His resurrection body, He said, "See My hands and My feet, that it is I Myself." In your resurrection body, you will be you. You will not be someone else.

Think of illnesses or injuries that you or your loved ones have suffered. What will it be like to have a new body that cannot be affected by cancer, illness, injury, or pain?

God, it seems everywhere I look, people are struggling with bodies that are broken, hurting, and tainted by the curse of sin. Thank You that in heaven, our bodies will be perfect!

What Was Jesus's Resurrection Body Like?

> I grant you that you may eat and drink at My table in My kingdom.
>
> —Luke 22:29–30

People have all kinds of questions about what our new bodies will be like. The best way to answer those questions is to look at the resurrection body of Jesus.

First of all, we will eat in our new bodies. When the resurrected Jesus appeared before His disciples, He was hungry and asked for something to eat. We will be hungry in heaven, and we will have plenty to eat. In Luke 22:29–30, Jesus said, "Just as My Father has granted Me a kingdom, I grant you that you may eat and drink at My table in My kingdom."

Second, we will wear clothes in heaven. Revelation 1:13 says Jesus in His resurrection body was "clothed in a robe reaching to the feet, and girded across His chest with a golden sash." Revelation 3:5 promises, "He who overcomes will thus be clothed in white garments." In Revelation 19:14, the second coming of Christ, we the church are pictured as coming with Christ, and we will be "clothed in fine linen, white and clean."

Third, we will retain our sexual identities in heaven. We will be male and female just as God created us. Some people point to Galatians 3:28—"[In Christ] there is neither male nor female"—to say there is no gender in heaven. But that verse refers to our equality right now before God. God makes no distinction between male and female in spiritual status. Galatians 3:28 is not talking about heaven. In Luke 24:16, Jesus was with His disciples on the road to Emmaus, "But their eyes were prevented from recognizing Him." How does that relate to gender? Obviously, when those disciples were talking to Jesus, He appeared to be just another man. He did not appear

In heaven, we will be the best version of ourselves we can imagine.

as some sexless alien. The disciples would have had a whole different conversation if that had been the case! In our resurrection bodies, we will retain our gender.

In heaven, we will be the best version of ourselves we can imagine. You will still be you, and the relationships you have here on earth with Christians will continue in heaven. You will know other people, they will know you, and you will enjoy perfect fellowship, untainted by sin. Now, that is something to look forward to in heaven!

What is the best version of yourself that you can imagine?

What are some things Jesus did in His resurrection body that encourage you about your future resurrection body?

Jesus, I am eager to be the best version of myself that I can imagine. Thank You that in heaven, I will enjoy perfect fellowship with You and with other Christians, untainted by sin.

Will Heaven Be the Same for Everyone?

Christ Jesus . . . is to judge the living and the dead.
—2 Timothy 4:1

Jim Marshall was a defensive lineman on the Minnesota Vikings' famed "Purple People Eaters" in the 1960s and '70s. Although Marshall was a Super Bowl champion, he is best known for the mistake he made on October 25, 1964. In a game with the San Francisco 49ers, Marshall saw a fumble, picked up the football, and began running the length of the field. Vikings players on the sidelines followed Marshall and began yelling . . . for him to run the other way! Marshall did not realize he was running toward his own end zone. Even though the Vikings ended up winning the game, Marshall is remembered not for his success but for his mistake. From that point on, he was known as Wrong Way Marshall.

Making it to the end zone is the goal in a football game, but making it to the right end zone is imperative for winning. It is the same way in the Christian life. Making it to heaven is the goal, but making it there to hear Jesus say, "Well done, good and faithful servant" is the key to ultimate victory.

If we have placed our faith in Jesus Christ, we are going to cross into the spiritual end zone of heaven, but some will make it there only after spending some time running in the wrong direction. Some Christians who make it into heaven will be celebrated by God for the way they played the game. Other

Christians will be evaluated by God for having done little to contribute to the success of the team.

Will heaven be the same for every Christian? The answer is no. It's a hard but inescapable truth: heaven will not be the same for every Christian. When "we . . . all stand before the judgment seat of God" (Rom. 14:10), some will receive great rewards and others will not. Not every Christian will have the same experience in heaven.

> *Heaven will not be the same for every Christian.*

How would you describe the right "end zone" in the Christian life? What can you do today that would make Jesus say, "Well done, good and faithful servant"?

God, I want to make it to the right spiritual end zone, without going in the wrong direction. Help me keep my focus on You and live obediently as I run in Your strength toward spiritual victory.

The Reality of Future Judgment

> It is appointed for men to die once and after this comes judgment.
>
> —Hebrews 9:27

The Bible is clear that everybody after death will be judged by God. Hebrews 9:27 says, "It is appointed for men to die once and after this comes judgment." We are all going to be judged.

In 2 Timothy 4:1, Paul talked about "Christ Jesus, who is to judge the living and the dead." Everyone, both Christians and non-Christians, will be judged by God, but we will not all be judged in a single judgment.

There is one judgment for non-Christians, called the great white throne judgment. At the end of the thousand-year reign of Christ on the earth, every unbeliever who has ever died will be raised and will stand before God at the great white throne judgment. Revelation 20:15 says, "If anyone's name was not found written in the book of life, he was thrown into the lake of fire." If you have not trusted in Christ as your Savior, then it does not matter how good you are. The only way to escape God's eternal judgment is by trusting in Christ as Savior before you die.

Both non-Christians and Christians have a judgment to face before God.

There is a very different judgment for Christians, called the judgment seat of Christ. This judgment results not in condemnation but in God's commendation for the lives we have lived for Christ. In 2 Corinthians 5:10, Paul said, "We must all appear before the judgment seat of Christ, so that each one may be recompensed for his deeds in the body, according to what he has done, whether good or bad." Both non-Christians and Christians have a judgment to face before God.

———

Why are many people afraid of being judged by God?
How can a person avoid God's wrath at the great white throne judgment?

Lord Jesus, You alone are worthy to judge the living and the dead. May You be pleased when I appear before You to be rewarded for how I lived for You in this life.

The Picture of the Christian's Judgment

We must all appear before the judgment seat of Christ, so that each one may be recompensed for his deeds in the body, according to what he has done, whether good or bad.

—2 Corinthians 5:10

In 2 Corinthians 5:10, Paul described a future judgment for Christians called "the judgment seat of Christ." What did Paul mean when he talked about the "judgment seat"?

During his second missionary journey, Paul spent eighteen months in Corinth, where many Jews, as well as Gentiles, came to faith in Christ. But not everybody was happy with him. Some were so incensed by what Paul was doing, especially by winning Jews to Christ, that they arrested him and dragged him before the Roman governor, Gallio. Acts 18:12 says, "While Gallio was proconsul of Achaia, the Jews with one accord rose up against Paul and brought him before the judgment seat." The word translated "judgment seat" is *bema* in Greek. It refers to the raised platform on which the governor would sit. Sometimes he would hand out rewards to successful athletes, and sometimes he would mete out justice. Both rewards and justice came from the official on this raised platform.

When the apostle Paul, in chains, was brought before Gallio, who was seated on the judgment seat, Gallio said,

If it were a matter of wrong or of vicious crime, O Jews, it would be reasonable for me to put up with you; but if there are questions about words and names and your own law, look after it yourselves; I am unwilling to be a judge of these matters. (vv. 14–15)

As Paul stood there, he undoubtedly realized, *This man has the power to extinguish my life.*

What gave Paul the courage to stand there, undaunted by the threats against him? As Paul looked at that judge, Gallio, I believe he thought, *One day I am going to stand in front of another Judge on the judgment seat, and I am going to have to give an account to Him for the way that I lived. I would much rather be found commended to Him than to this human judge, who has no power other than what God gives him.*

> *Paul had this mindset:* I am going to live my life to please the true Judge.

Paul had this mindset: *I am going to live my life to please the true Judge, because one day we must all appear before the judgment seat of Christ, every one of us.*

How can the judgment seat of Christ inspire Christians to live obedient and holy lives?

In what ways will the knowledge of this future event affect your choices today?

Jesus, Your Word says that one day all Christians will have to give an account to You for the way we lived. Help me stay obedient and faithful until the day I appear before You, the true Judge.

The Difference between the Christian's Judgment and the Non-Christian's Judgment

> There is now no condemnation for those who are in Christ Jesus.
>
> —Romans 8:1

What is the difference between the Christian's judgment and the non-Christian's judgment? The judgment seat of Christ is for the commendation of believers, while the great white throne judgment is for the condemnation of unbelievers. The result of the judgment seat of Christ will be eternal rewards, while the result of the great white throne judgment will be God's eternal punishment.

Only those who are saved will be at the judgment seat of Christ. The judgment seat of Christ is not to determine whether somebody goes to heaven or hell. If you are a Christian, that has already been decided by your faith in Jesus. If you wait until after you die to choose whether you are going to heaven or hell, you will have waited too long. That is a decision you make now by placing your faith in Jesus Christ.

Only those who are saved will be at the judgment seat of Christ.

The moment you trust in Jesus as your Savior, you are justified in the sight of God. Romans 5:1 says, "Having been justified by faith, we have peace with God through our Lord

Jesus Christ." That word *justified* means "to be declared righteous." It does not matter what you have done; when you trust in Jesus as Savior, He washes it away, and God declares you "not guilty" before Him. When you become a Christian, God no longer sees your sin; He sees the righteousness of His Son, Jesus Christ. That is what it means to be justified: to be in a right relationship with God. Romans 8:1 says, "There is now no condemnation for those who are in Christ Jesus." If you are a Christian and have been forgiven by God, then you never have to worry that one day God is going to condemn you.

———

What are some differences between the great white throne judgment and the judgment seat of Christ?

Why do you think Satan tempts Christians to fear that God will condemn them?

Lord Jesus, I'm so grateful there is no condemnation for those who trust You as Savior! Give me Your peace today, knowing that I will never be condemned for sins You have already forgiven.

Our Ambition Is to Be Pleasing to Christ

We also have as our ambition, whether at home or absent, to be pleasing to Him.

—2 Corinthians 5:9

After you become a Christian, you no longer have to worry about God's condemnation, but you still need to be mindful of His evaluation of your life. That is why 2 Corinthians 5:10 says, "We [Christians] must all appear before the judgment seat of Christ." I've checked the Greek text, and "all" means *all*! Every Christian will stand before the judgment seat of Christ—no exceptions, exclusions, or exemptions.

Each of us will appear before the Lord for an evaluation to receive whatever reward is appropriate. That is why the apostle Paul wrote, "We also have as our ambition, whether at home or absent, to be pleasing to Him" (v. 9). Knowing that we will stand before Christ's evaluation, we ought to have as our one aim in life to be pleasing to God.

Knowing that we will stand before Christ's evaluation, we ought to have as our one aim in life to be pleasing to God.

When does this evaluation of Christians take place? It does not happen the moment we die. Although the Bible does not tell us exactly when the judgment seat of Christ will occur, I believe it happens at the rapture of the church, at the beginning of the seven years of tribulation on the earth, when all living Christians are immediately transported to the presence of the Lord and Christians who have died are resurrected to eternal life.

While no single verse indicates that the judgment seat of Christ occurs immediately after the rapture, a number of factors point to this conclusion. Revelation 4:10 occurs before the tribulation, and the twenty-four elders in heaven are portrayed as having already received their rewards from Jesus Christ. They are wearing their crowns and praising God. The twenty-four elders in heaven represent the church, so apparently Christians have already been rewarded at the beginning of the tribulation. Additionally, Revelation 19:8 says, "It was given to her [the church] to clothe herself in fine linen, bright and clean; for the fine linen is the righteous acts of the saints." Apparently by the time the church, the bride of Christ, returns to earth with Jesus at the second coming, we will have already received our rewards, as evidenced by wearing "fine linen, bright and clean," which is "the righteous acts of the saints." Both of these facts imply that the evaluation of Christians' lives has already occurred.

———————

If you are a Christian, which future judgment will you face: condemnation or evaluation?

How does the knowledge that you will one day stand before Christ's evaluation affect the way you live today?

> *Lord, help me to remember that everything I do in my Christian life has eternal consequences. May I choose to live today, and every day, in a way that pleases You.*

The Importance of Good Works in the Christian's Life

> By grace you have been saved through faith; and that not of yourselves, it is the gift of God; not as a result of works, so that no one may boast.
>
> —Ephesians 2:8–9

What is the importance of good works in a Christian's life? Do our works really matter to God?

Many Christians are confused about the importance of obedience to God in this life. "My good works are worthless to God," they mistakenly claim. While it is true that we are saved by God's grace apart from our works, God rewards us as Christians based on our works.

We need to distinguish between the value of our good works before we are saved and the value of our good works after we are saved. What is the value of your good works to God before you are a Christian? Zero. Zilch. Nada. Isaiah 64:6 says the best you and I can do before we are saved is like "a filthy garment" to God. That is why Ephesians 2:8–9 says, "By grace you have been saved through faith; and that not of yourselves, it is the gift of God; not as a result of works, so that no one may boast."

While our good works are worthless in securing us a place in heaven, they are integral in determining our experience in heaven.

God does not allow us to work for our salvation. If He allowed us to work for our salvation, then salvation would be something He owed us, and God refuses to owe any person anything. Salvation is a measure of God's grace to us. The value of our good works before we are saved is nothing. We cannot earn our salvation.

However, there is value to our works after our salvation. While our good works are worthless in securing us a place in heaven, they are integral in determining our experience in heaven.

Think about some of the "good works" you did before you were saved. According to Isaiah 64:6, how does God view those good works? Why didn't God allow you to work for your salvation?

God, thank You for assuring me that my salvation is based completely on Your grace, not my works. Help me to honor You today through acts of love, service, and obedience to You.

Do Our Works Really Matter?

> We are His workmanship, created in Christ Jesus
> for good works, which God prepared beforehand
> so that we would walk in them.
>
> —Ephesians 2:10

The apostle Paul drew a distinction between our works *before* salvation and our works *after* salvation. This is what he said about our works before salvation: "For by grace you have been saved through faith; and that not of yourselves, it is the gift of God; not as a result of works, so that no one may boast" (Eph. 2:8–9). We are not saved by our good works.

However, this is what Paul said about our works after salvation: "For we are His workmanship, created in Christ Jesus for good works, which God prepared beforehand so that we would walk in them" (v. 10).

Before we became a Christian, our works were sufficient to condemn us before God. But after we are saved, our good works are sufficient to commend us to God. That is why Paul said in 2 Corinthians 5:9–10,

> We also have as our ambition, whether at home or absent, to be pleasing to Him. For we must all appear before the judgment seat of Christ, so that each one may be recompensed for his deeds in the body, according to what he has done, whether good or bad.

Now, the phrase "good or bad" is an unfortunate translation, because it makes us think that judgment is based on whether they are morally good or morally bad. But that is not what the word means. The word *good* here refers to that which endures, something that is lasting. The word *bad* does not refer to something that is morally bad; it means "worthless."

The judgment seat of Christ does not determine whether we go to heaven or hell; that was settled the

Did we spend our lives on things that had eternal consequence—or did we spend our lives on things that were worthless?

moment of our salvation. This is a judgment of rewards. And the standard by which you and I as Christians are going to be judged is this: Did we spend our lives on things that had eternal consequence—or did we spend our lives on things that were worthless?

Are you spending your life on things that have eternal consequence, or are you focusing on things that are limited to this world and, ultimately, worthless?

How can you focus on eternal things today?

Lord, help me live today in light of eternity. Instead of spending all my energy on temporary things of this world, help me focus on eternal things, such as sharing the gospel, strengthening the church, and living in obedience to You.

The Value of Our Works after Our Salvation

> If any man builds on the foundation with gold, silver, precious stones, wood, hay, straw, each man's work will become evident.
>
> —1 Corinthians 3:12–13

Not everything we do in life is either morally good or morally bad. For example, there is nothing morally good or bad about going to the mall. And there is nothing morally good or bad about purchasing a suit of clothes or buying a car. A lot of things we do in life are not morally good or bad, but that is not the standard used to determine our rewards at the judgment seat of Christ.

The standard God will use to evaluate our good works after salvation is this: Does it have value in the big scheme of things?

The standard God will use to evaluate our good works after salvation is this: Does it have value in the big scheme of things?

Will your life be judged as having substance, being invested in growing God's kingdom, or will your life be judged as being inconsequential and worthless?

In 1 Corinthians 3:12, Paul described a life that endures as one that is built with "gold, silver, precious stones." A life that is worthless is one that is constructed with "wood, hay, straw." Now, there is nothing wrong with wood, hay, and straw. They are useful for some purposes, but ultimately, they blow away. Paul said that is the judgment Christians will face: How did we invest our time? How did we invest our money? It is not that we invested in bad things, but were they worthless things compared to the kingdom of God? That is what will be evaluated at the judgment seat of Christ.

———

How are you investing your time?

How are you investing your money?

What can you do to invest in eternal things and focus on expanding the kingdom of God?

Lord, thank You for giving me so many things to enjoy in this life. Help me to build my life with "gold, silver, precious stones"—things that bring You glory and last for eternity.

Nothing Will Be Hidden

> Nothing is hidden that will not become evident, nor anything secret that will not be known and come to light.
>
> —Luke 8:17

When I think about God's evaluation of our lives, I think about an embarrassing evaluation I had some years ago at my annual physical exam at a clinic in Dallas. Part of the examination involved determining my body fat. The doctor's assistant instructed me to remove my clothes and get into a basket to be submerged into what was appropriately called "the fat tank." As I held my breath underwater, the doctor calculated my percentage of body fat. Next, the doctor took this little torture device and started pinching various parts of my body to measure my body fat using a different method. That was humiliating. As I stood there, I was filled with regrets. I regretted every chocolate chip cookie I had ever eaten. I regretted every time I rolled over in bed instead of getting on the treadmill. I regretted those midnight trips to the freezer for ice cream. Everything I had done was on view to that doctor. Standing there without a stitch of clothing on, being pinched, poked, and prodded while my doctor frowned, scowled, and grinned, caused me to think one thought: *He knows everything!*

But the worst part was putting my clothes back on and sitting down for the evaluation. He brought in his folder and said, "Now we're going to talk about your health." He started on a positive note. He commended me for the good things I was doing: my exercise, the bran flakes I gagged down every morning. Then his smile turned to a frown as he said, "You need to shave some points off your cholesterol, and your blood pressure isn't exactly where we would like it." He gave a critique and evaluation of my life.

The judgment seat of Christ is going to be an honest evaluation of everything we have done.

That is what the judgment seat of Christ is going to be like. The judgment seat of Christ is going to be an honest evaluation of everything we have done, whether it is good, lasting, eternal, or worthless. In Luke 8:17, Jesus said, "Nothing is hidden that will not become evident, nor anything secret that will not be known and come to light."

Have you ever gone through an evaluation, perhaps by a doctor, teacher, or boss?

What was the result of that evaluation?

How does that experience help you understand the judgment seat of Christ?

Lord God, I realize that everything I do in this life will someday come to light. May I live today with an awareness that my choices as a Christian will have eternal consequences at the judgment seat of Christ.

The Significance of Our Works

> If any man's work which he has built on it remains, he will receive a reward. If any man's work is burned up, he will suffer loss; but he himself will be saved, yet so as through fire.
>
> —1 Corinthians 3:14–15

At the judgment seat of Christ, there are two criteria God is going to use to judge the kind of lives you and I have built.

The first criterion of judgment is the significance of our works. If we spend our time, talents, and treasures here on earth pursuing our own agendas, then that is like building a house of wood, hay, or straw (1 Cor. 3:12). I am not talking about a life that is built on evil; I am talking about a worthless life, a life that is focused on ourselves.

The first criterion of judgment is the significance of our works.

What happens at the judgment seat of Christ if your life is built on your own profit, power, or pleasure? It's not like the story of the three little pigs where Jesus will huff and puff and blow your house down—instead, He just burns it up. That's what Paul was saying in 1 Corinthians 3:12–15. Nothing will last. It will be consumed by fire.

On the other hand, you can build your life with more durable materials: gold, silver, and precious stones. This is a life built around glorifying God, making Him look good no matter what your daily responsibilities are. It's a life built around sharing Christ with as many people as possible. It's a life built around giving up some temporary pleasures and perks to invest your money in God's kingdom. Those things really matter to God and represent a life built with gold, silver, and precious stones (v. 12).

In 1 Corinthians 3:14–15, Paul said, "If any man's work which he has built on it remains, he will receive a reward. If any man's work is burned up, he will suffer loss; but he himself will be saved, yet so as through fire." If you are a Christian and your life is judged to be worthless, you will still get into heaven, but you will smell of smoke.

Which activities in your life are focused on yourself?
Which activities in your life are focused on glorifying God?

God, help me to arrange my activities and priorities today around things that really matter to You and represent a life built with gold, silver, and precious stones.

The Motives of Our Works

> The Lord . . . [will] bring to light the things hidden in the darkness and disclose the motives of men's hearts; and then each man's praise will come to him from God.
>
> —1 Corinthians 4:5

At the judgment seat of Christ, what are the criteria that God is going to use to judge the kind of lives you and I have built? The first criterion of judgment will be the significance of our works. After you became a Christian, did you spend your time, talents, and treasures here on earth pursuing your own agenda, or did you build your life around glorifying and serving God?

The second criterion of the judgment seat of Christ is the motives of our works. Sometimes why we do what we do is as important as what we do. In 1 Corinthians 4:5, Paul said, "The Lord . . . [will] bring to light the things hidden in the darkness and disclose the motives of men's hearts; and then each man's praise will come to him from God."

God cares about our motives. If you give money to God's work in order to be able to brag to others, that does not count for gold; it counts as wood (1 Cor. 3:12). If you are diligent in sharing your faith so you can brag about how many people are in the kingdom because of you, that is not silver; that is hay. Our motives really do matter before God. Proverbs 16:2 says, "All the ways of a man are clean in his own sight, but the LORD weighs the motives."

You might ask, "Isn't living to earn rewards a selfish motive? Isn't it self-centered to earn all these rewards to have a better spot in heaven than other people?" Somebody has said that selfishness is trying to gain more at somebody else's expense.

But did you know that it is possible to gain more at God's expense? God does not have a finite amount of resources so that if you take some from Him, He then has less. God has an inexhaustible supply of riches. When God rewards you, His net worth is not diminished

Working for rewards is a sign of what God values most in our lives, and that is faith.

one iota. In fact, when you think about it, working for rewards is a sign of what God values most in our lives, and that is faith.

How would you describe your motives for the good works you do as a Christian?

Is there any area in which you need to change your motive?

God, Your Word says that above all else, You value faith. As I pursue a life of obedience, help me examine my motives to make sure that everything I do brings honor and glory to You.

The Christian's Crowns

> My reward is with Me, to render to every man according to what he has done.
>
> —Revelation 22:12

Some Christians will receive rewards at the judgment seat of Christ. People sometimes say, "That is not fair. Shouldn't everybody be treated equally?" It does not work that way in heaven. We are going to be rewarded for what we have done. In Revelation 22:12, Jesus said, "My reward is with Me, to render to every man according to what he has done." God cares what you and I do in this life.

The rewards we receive at the judgment seat of Christ are sometimes referred to in the Bible as crowns. The Bible describes at least five crowns as possible rewards in heaven.

The Bible describes at least five crowns as possible rewards in heaven.

First, there is the imperishable crown (1 Cor. 9:25). This is the reward for living a disciplined, Spirit-controlled life.

Second, there is the crown of exaltation, or the crown of rejoicing (1 Thess. 2:19–20). This is a reward for those who have dedicated themselves to evangelism and discipleship.

Third, there is the crown of righteousness (2 Tim. 4:8). This is a reward for those who live obediently in anticipation of Christ's return.

Fourth, there is the crown of life (James 1:12; Rev. 2:10). This is a crown reserved for those who endure specific trials without denying Christ or losing their faith.

Fifth, there is the crown of glory (1 Pet. 5:4). This is a crown that is reserved for those who faithfully and sacrificially serve Christ's church, especially pastors who teach God's Word and lead their congregations in a way that is pleasing to God.

Some people believe these are literal crowns that we will wear. Others say we will cast them before the throne of God, as the twenty-four elders do in Revelation 4:10. But the fact is, people will have different experiences in heaven. While we all will praise God for our salvation, that does not mean everybody's experience is going to be identical.

Which of these five crowns do you hope to receive at the judgment seat of Christ?

What specific things can you do to receive that reward someday?

God, help me examine my spiritual life today. Show me any changes I need to make to be faithful to You and live in light of these eternal rewards.

Special Privileges in Heaven

> In this way the entrance into the eternal kingdom of
> our Lord and Savior Jesus Christ will be abundantly
> supplied to you.
>
> —2 Peter 1:11

Are the crowns that we receive at the judgment seat of Christ literal crowns? Some people believe they are. Of course, you have to wonder, if you have more than one or two crowns, how is that going to work walking around heaven wearing four or five? Other people say, "We are going to cast our crowns before the throne of God, so it does not matter." I believe that these crowns may be literal crowns, and indeed we may cast them before the throne of God as a sign of worship, but that does not negate the fact that these crowns represent real, tangible rewards that will extend throughout eternity.

What kind of rewards will Christians receive? Our rewards will include special privileges in heaven. When our daughters were young, we used to take them to Disneyland. If you have ever been to "The Happiest Place on Earth," you know that for a basic price, everybody gets in the park to ride the rides. However, if you want to pay more, you get to do extra things. You get to go into the park an hour early, before the crowds come. You get to go to the front of the line for rides. If you really want to pay an arm and a leg,

These crowns represent real, tangible rewards that will extend throughout eternity.

you can even have breakfast with Mickey and Minnie. It is a special privilege for those who are willing to do a little more.

Heaven is going to be that way. The experience of heaven is not going to be the same for everybody. The Bible teaches that some people are going to receive a special welcome from God, like a ticker tape parade, according to 2 Peter 1:11. Some people are going to have special access to the tree of life, according to Revelation 2:7. Some people will even have special treatment by Jesus Himself. Jesus is not going to treat everybody the same in heaven, according to Luke 12:37.

What kinds of special treatment in heaven does the Bible describe? What is the difference between working for your salvation and working for these special privileges in heaven?

Lord, help me to be neither unconcerned nor overly concerned with my heavenly rewards. Instead, keep me focused on honoring and serving You in this life. I trust You to evaluate my works as a Christian and assign my rewards in heaven.

Special Positions in Heaven

> You were faithful with a few things, I will put you
> in charge of many things.
>
> —Matthew 25:21

In 2 Corinthians 5:10, Paul said, "We must all appear before the judgment seat of Christ, so that each one may be recompensed for his deeds in the body, according to what he has done, whether good or bad." The Bible says there are three kinds of heavenly rewards that these crowns represent. As we have seen, first, these rewards include special privileges. Jesus is not going to treat everybody the same in heaven.

Second, these rewards entail special positions in heaven. Those who are faithful in this life will be put in charge and have moral responsibilities in heaven. In the parable of the talents, Jesus commended those who were faithful: "Well done, good and faithful [servant]. You were faithful with a few things, I will put you in charge of many things; enter into the joy of your master" (Matt. 25:21).

Those who are faithful in this life will be put in charge and have moral responsibilities in heaven.

Third, these rewards entail special praise in heaven. Can you look back in your life and recall when somebody said something especially encouraging to you? Maybe a parent said, "I am so proud of you." Maybe an employer said, "You are doing such a great job; we could not make it in this company without you." You hold on to those things, don't you? You replay them over and over in your mind. If we can get that excited about what a parent or an employer says to us, think about what it will be like to stand at the judgment seat of Christ and see Jesus smile and say, "Well done, good and faithful servant." That is a reward worth working for.

Think of a time when an authority figure said something encouraging to you. How did that make you feel?

How do you think that will compare to the day when Jesus says to you, "Well done, good and faithful servant"?

Lord Jesus, I want to serve You faithfully in this life. Help me get rid of any impure motives or earthly distractions that lead me away from eternal things. I look forward to the day when I will hear You say, "Well done, good and faithful servant."

Regrets for Some Christians

> Abide in Him, so that when He appears, we may
> have confidence and not shrink away from Him in
> shame at His coming.
>
> —1 John 2:28

Someday, all Christians are going to stand before the judgment seat of Christ. One possible outcome of this judgment is reward. Some Christians will receive special privileges, positions, and praise. The other possible outcome is regret. Some Christians will stand before Jesus in shame.

In 1 John 2:28, John said, "Abide in Him, so that when He appears, we may have confidence and not shrink away from Him in shame at His coming." Some Christians will stand before the judgment seat of Christ, and as Jesus evaluates their lives, they will regret what could have been theirs had they been more faithful in their service of Christ. Paul wrote about that in 1 Corinthians 3:15: "If any man's work is burned up, he will suffer loss; but he himself will be saved, yet so as through fire."

To overemphasize the regret at the judgment seat of Christ is to turn heaven into hell, but to underemphasize it is to make obedience in this life inconsequential.

You may say, "I thought heaven was supposed to be a place of complete, unending joy. How can there be regret in heaven? What about Revelation 21:4, which says, 'He will wipe away every tear from their eyes'?" Yes, God is going to do that for us. Revelation 21:4 occurs after the judgment seat of Christ, after the new heaven and new earth. And while God will wipe away every tear, He will not wipe away the consequences of failing to win rewards at the judgment seat of Christ. Those consequences last for eternity.

We have to be careful. To overemphasize the regret at the judgment seat of Christ is to turn heaven into hell, but to underemphasize it is to make obedience in this life inconsequential. Rewards will matter. Rewards in heaven are about trading the temporal for the eternal.

Is it possible to experience joy and regret at the same time?

What practical steps can you take today to make sure you don't stand before the judgment seat of Christ with regrets?

Jesus, open my eyes to the eternal significance of the choices I make every day. Give me the courage to make changes in my life that will minimize any regrets when I stand before You.

How Can I Prepare for My Journey to Heaven?

> Truly I say to you, unless you are converted and become like children, you will not enter the kingdom of heaven.
>
> —Matthew 18:3

My family recently traveled to London, and the trip was uneventful except for one mistake I made: I forgot to pack any extra socks. By the fourth day, I broke down and bought some cheap socks at a local store. Now, that mistake had no lasting consequences. However, failing to prepare for the trip we are taking after we die can have devastating and unending consequences.

How can we prepare for our journey to heaven? The first step is the most foundational, and that is to make sure we have a valid passport. To travel to most countries, we need a passport. No passport, no entry into that country.

Failing to prepare for the trip we are taking after we die can have devastating and unending consequences.

I learned about the importance of passports years ago. When I was a youth minister at the church I now pastor, our student choir traveled to the Soviet Union. It was during the Cold War, and the atmosphere was oppressive. Frankly, we couldn't wait to get out of there. Finally, the day of our departure arrived. At the airport, I watched as our students went through passport control one by one, with expressions of relief as they passed from bondage to freedom. As the group leader, I waited until everyone else was on the other side to pass through myself. I reached inside my coat pocket for my passport—and it was missing.

I frantically searched for the missing document with no success. I explained to the Soviet agent my predicament. Trust me, he could not have cared less! No passport, no exit.

After watching me sweat for a while, a friend of mine held up my passport, which he had taken as a joke. I can assure you that after more than thirty-five years, my wife still does not think it was funny! I will never forget the relief I felt as I finally settled in my seat on the plane.

The absolute panic I felt that night pales in comparison to the terror that will grip the hearts of those who will be denied entrance into heaven because they lack the proper "passport." As they stand at heaven's entrance expecting to be welcomed into God's presence, they will instead hear these words: "I never knew you; depart from Me" (Matt. 7:23).

Have you prepared for your future journey to heaven?
When you stand at the entrance of heaven, what do you think God will say to you?

Lord, I don't know exactly when You will call me away from this life. Help me to fulfill my responsibilities in this world faithfully while also being diligent in preparing for the next life.

Our Spiritual Passport to Heaven

> Having been justified by faith, we have peace with
> God through our Lord Jesus Christ.
>
> —Romans 5:1

What is the spiritual passport we need to get into heaven? It's not a heart stamped "Catholic." If your heart is stamped "Catholic," you are not going to make it into heaven. It's not a heart stamped "Baptist." If your heart is stamped "Baptist," you are not getting into heaven. Nor are you going to be welcomed into heaven if your heart is stamped "Church of Christ," or any other denomination. Only a heart stamped "Forgiven" will be welcomed into heaven. That's all that matters: being forgiven of our sins. No other stamp makes a difference in the presence of God.

The Bible has a word for being forgiven. It's the New Testament word *justified*, which means "to be declared righteous." *Justified* is a legal term that refers to what God does for us when we trust in Christ as Savior. When we put our faith in Christ alone for our salvation, God justifies us—He declares us "not guilty" based on what Christ did for us on the cross. Romans 5:1 says, "Having been justified by faith, we have peace with God through our Lord Jesus Christ." The only way we are allowed into heaven is by being forgiven of our sins.

The only way we are allowed into heaven is by being forgiven of our sins.

172

There are not many ways to heaven; there is only one way to heaven, and that is through faith in Christ. I realize that is an unpopular statement today. Many people think there are other routes to heaven. Billionaire Warren Buffett donated 85 percent of his net worth to charity, saying, "There is more than one way to get to heaven, but this is a great way."[1] I commend Buffett for his generosity, but he will be surprised when he discovers that he cannot donate his way to heaven. There is only one way to heaven, and that is through faith in Jesus Christ.

––––––––––

What "stamp" is on your spiritual passport?
Have you been forgiven of your sins through your faith in Jesus Christ as your Savior?

God, thank You for making it clear in Your Word that the only way to be welcomed into heaven is through faith in Your Son, Jesus Christ. Give me the courage to speak Your truth and opportunities to share the gospel today.

What Does It Mean to "Believe" in Jesus?

> God has given us eternal life, and this life is in His Son.
>
> —1 John 5:11

How can you make sure that when you stand at the entrance of heaven, God is going to look at your heart and welcome you into His presence? The book of 1 John was written in order that people might know for sure their eternal destination. In 1 John 5:11–13, the apostle wrote,

> God has given us eternal life, and this life is in His Son. He who has the Son has the life; he who does not have the Son of God does not have the life. These things I have written to you who believe in the name of the Son of God, so that you may know that you have eternal life.

Who are the people who know they have eternal life? Those who "believe in the name of the Son of God."

That word *believe* does not mean an intellectual assent to a certain set of facts about Jesus. You can believe all the things about Jesus correctly: that He was the Son of God, that He died on the cross for the sins of the world, and that He rose again on the third day. You can believe all those things and still go to hell when you die. The Bible says even "the demons also believe" those things (James 2:19).

To believe means "to trust in, to cling to, to put your whole weight upon." To believe in Jesus means to come to that place in your life where you realize you cannot save yourself. You trust in what Christ did for you by dying on the cross and receiving the punishment that God intended for each of us. Only by clinging to, trusting in, and putting your whole weight upon Jesus Christ is your heart stamped "Forgiven," and you are welcomed in the presence of God.

If we place our faith in Jesus Christ, we can know with absolute certainty that we are going to be welcomed into heaven.

Notice what John said: "These things I have written to you . . . so that you may know that you have eternal life" (1 John 5:13). God does not want us to face death uncertain about our future. If we place our faith in Jesus Christ, we can know with absolute certainty that we are going to be welcomed into heaven.

Do you know for certain that you have eternal life?
Why or why not?
What is the difference between believing facts about Jesus and believing in Jesus?

Lord Jesus, I want to be sure that when I stand before the entrance of heaven, You will welcome me with open arms. Help me cling to, trust in, and put the whole weight of my life on You today.

Live with a Destination Mindset

> Our citizenship is in heaven, from which also we
> eagerly wait for a Savior, the Lord Jesus Christ.
> —Philippians 3:20

A few years ago, Northwest Airlines came up with a promotional gimmick they called "Mystery Fares." For $59, you could buy a ticket for a weekend trip on Northwest Airlines. The catch was you didn't find out where you were going until you got to the airport. Interestingly, thousands of people bought into this "Mystery Fare" idea. They reasoned, "It's only $59 for a couple of days—there's no great risk in that." Most people were happy. A few weren't thrilled with their destination, but overall, the promotion was a success.

Now, mystery fares can be fun. They can be interesting, but there is one day in your life you don't want to be holding a mystery fare ticket, and that's the day of your death. To face eternity without knowing with absolute certainty where you are headed is a risk that no sane person would take.

How can you prepare for your journey to heaven? First, you need to have a valid spiritual passport: a heart that is stamped "Forgiven." Another practical step to prepare for heaven is to live with a destination mindset. The fact is, we do not know when our departure to heaven will be, so we face an unusual responsibility of preparing for our trip to the next world while still living in this world. God calls us to be residents of two worlds: the next world and this world.

Make no mistake about it: our true citizenship is in heaven. Philippians 3:20 says, "Our citizenship is in heaven, from which also we eagerly wait for a Savior, the Lord Jesus Christ." Our real citizenship is in the new country we are headed toward.

Nevertheless, God has left us here as well, and He has given us certain responsibilities. We have responsibilities with the family God has entrusted to us. We have responsibilities at work. And, of course, our greatest responsibility is

> *We are preparing for the next world while living in this world.*

to be "ambassadors for Christ" (2 Cor. 5:20), to be God's representatives urging people to be reconciled to God through faith in Jesus. We are preparing for the next world while living in this world.

———

How can you live in this world without becoming entangled in it? What steps can you take today to be an effective resident of this world and also a faithful citizen of heaven?

God, while I wait for You to call me to my true home in heaven, help me complete the assignments You have entrusted to me in this world. Show me how to prepare for the next world while also living in this one.

Living in One World, Preparing for Another

> Set your mind on the things above, not on the things that are on earth.
>
> —Colossians 3:2

Admittedly, it is difficult to live in more than one place at one time. I remember when Amy and I were called to the pastorate of my first church in Eastland, Texas, more than thirty years ago. We traveled to that small congregation to preach in view of a call. The congregation got to meet with me, listen to me, and then vote on whether they wanted to call me as pastor. After I preached my trial sermon, they ushered Amy and me into a small room and fed us pie while the congregation deliberated. I will never forget the exhilaration I felt when we learned they had voted to call me as their pastor. We could barely sleep that night as we contemplated the adventure before us.

However, the next morning, reality set in. We drove back to Dallas and spent the next month wrapping up our ministry there. For that month, I tried to concentrate on doing the best job I could in Dallas, but my heart was already at my new church. While we were working here, we were thinking about there. We were living in both worlds. During that final month in Dallas, I had more motivation to work hard than I had experienced during the previous seven years—mainly because I knew my time in Dallas was limited and I wanted to leave

178

things in good shape! Focusing on "there" (my new church in Eastland) profoundly impacted my life "here" (in Dallas).

That is a good illustration of what God has called us to do. We are to be thinking about and preparing for heaven, but we still have work to do here. The Bible talks about that here/there mentality. In Hebrews 11:13, the writer said we are "strangers and exiles"

> *The more we focus on heaven, the more effective we become on earth.*

on earth. In Colossians 3:2, Paul said, "Set your mind on the things above, not on the things that are on earth." But here is the irony: the more we focus on heaven, the more effective we become on earth.

Have you ever anticipated something new, such as going to college, getting married, or starting a job?

How did your exciting new future affect the way you lived in your current reality?

What can you do today to prepare for your exciting new future in heaven?

Lord, help me prepare for my journey to heaven by taking the necessary steps in this world while I await my future destination, anticipating that day with joy and hope.

Refuse to Allow Your Departure to Paralyze You with Fear

My times are in Your hand.
—Psalm 31:15

How do you prepare for your journey to heaven? Refuse to allow your departure to paralyze you with fear.

As the departure date approached for our recent family trip to London, I had a number of emotions. One was anticipation of going to a foreign city and seeing many of the sites I had read about. One was excitement about spending a few quality days with my family. I also felt a sense of urgency from a need to wrap up everything here before I left on my trip. But do you know one emotion I never felt? Fear. There was nothing to fear about my trip to London. Why should I be fearful about a place I had invested in and prepared to go to? It is the same way about our departure to heaven. There is no reason for us as Christians to fear our journey that we are all going to make to heaven.

Christians never need to fear our departure to heaven.

Yet if we are honest, a lot of Christians do fear that journey to heaven. Maybe you are one of those. One reason they fear it is they do not know much about it. That is why it is important to understand what God has planned for us. Christians never need to fear our departure to heaven.

If you are a Christian, you can bank on this: you will not depart this world one second before God's departure time for you. Death is never premature. No Christian leaves this world one second before God's appointed time.

Have you ever been afraid of dying?
How could focusing on the hope of heaven help you overcome that fear?

Lord God, You know exactly how many days You have ordained for me to live in this world. My death, whenever it happens, will be exactly at Your appointed time. Help me to trust in Your purpose for my life and to make the most of the days You have planned for me.

Nobody Dies before Their Appointed Time

> We have obtained an inheritance, having been predestined according to His purpose who works all things after the counsel of His will.
>
> —Ephesians 1:11

Throughout the Bible, we see the truth that God has ordained the years, months, days, and seconds of every person's life. For example, consider what the apostle Paul said in Acts 13:36: "David, after he had served the purpose of God in his own generation, fell asleep." When did David die? He died after he had fulfilled God's purpose for him. That is true for you and me as well. Nobody dies before their appointed time.

You may ask, "What about those who seem to die prematurely, such as a teenager in a car accident or a young mother who leaves her small children behind?" From God's perspective, no one dies prematurely. The psalmist declared, "My times are in Your hand" (Ps. 31:15). God determines our days and numbers our years. In his great sermon at Pentecost, the apostle Peter said that even Jesus's death occurred according to "the predetermined plan and foreknowledge of God" (Acts 2:23). Just as the day of Jesus's death was determined by God, so is the day of your death.

God had a plan for Jesus's life. His plan included the date of Jesus's birth in Bethlehem—and the day of His death on Calvary. And that same God has an immutable, unchangeable plan for your life. He has written down the day of your birth, and He has written down the day of your death.

In Ephesians 1:11, Paul wrote that all things in our lives—including death—have been "predestined according to His purpose who works all things after the counsel of His will." There are no accidents in your life. No death catches God off guard. He has everything under control. Everything, including the day of your death, is according to the counsel of His will. Those who die in faith—whether they are nine or ninety—lived exactly the number of years God prescribed for them.

Your life is in God's hands.

Somebody has said, "Every person is immortal until his or her work on earth is done." Doesn't that give you confidence to know there are no mistakes in God's plan? Your life is in God's hands. And that's why no Christian needs to fear his or her departure from this world.

Have you ever been shocked or surprised by the news of someone who seemed to die "prematurely"?

How did today's Bible passages help you understand God's sovereignty and plan for our lives?

God, along with the psalmist, I declare, "My times are in Your hand." You are sovereign, and nothing ever catches You off guard. When tragic and unexpected deaths leave me with legitimate questions and grief, help me cling to the truth that You are in control and have a purpose.

Death Is a Gate That Leads to Freedom

Flesh and blood cannot inherit the kingdom of God;
nor does the perishable inherit the imperishable.
—1 Corinthians 15:50

Why should we as Christians not fear our death? Death is a necessary transition from this world to the next world.

As I mentioned earlier, I once took a group of youth choir members on a trip to the former Soviet Union. When the day of our departure came and I presented my passport to the Soviet guard at the airport, I had to go through a metal gate to travel from one place to the next place. As that gate opened up at passport control, did I dread going through it? No, I almost ran through that gate. I was elated to be escaping the tyranny of the Soviet Union and heading toward freedom.

The Bible says death is like that gate. It is a narrow passageway we must go through to leave the tyranny of this world and experience the freedom God has planned for us. Why would we fear going through that gate? It is what leads us to everything God has planned for us.

Death is necessary for the Christian.

The apostle Paul said it this way in 1 Corinthians 15:50: "Flesh and blood cannot inherit the kingdom of God; nor does the perishable inherit the imperishable." Death is necessary for the Christian. One reason is we need a change of clothes in order to live and exist in the new heaven

184

and new earth. This body we are wearing right now is perfectly designed for our current world. But we have to change clothes if we are going to go to heaven. That is what death is.

———

In what ways is death like passing through a gate from tyranny to freedom?

Why is death a necessary part of our journey to heaven?

Lord, I know the freedom that awaits me in heaven is far better than anything I can imagine. Give me a healthy perspective on death as a gate that leads to my heavenly home.

Death Is a Necessary Transition to Heaven

Blessed are you who weep now, for you shall laugh.
—Luke 6:21

Some futurists predict that in the near future, many citizens of earth will be living on Mars. I do not know if that is going to happen or not, but what I do know is this: If I am going to live on Mars, the clothes I am wearing, which are fine for life on earth, are not going to work on Mars. I'll have to put on a spacesuit in order to exist in that other world.

The same thing is true for us spiritually. This body we are wearing right now is perfectly designed for this world. But we have to change clothes if we are going to go to heaven. That is what death is. Death is a change of clothes. The Greek word for death, *thanatos*, means "separation." At death, our spirits are separated from our bodies. Our old bodies are left behind so we can put on a new body that is designed for the new world. Why should we dread that? We ought to look forward to it. I mean, do you know any man who would mind exchanging his ripped-up pajamas for a new Brioni suit? Do you know any woman who would pass on exchanging her bathrobe for a Chanel dress? I don't think so!

That is exactly the kind of exchange we make at death. God has invited every Christian to a magnificent location for which we must be properly dressed, and He has provided the appropriate spiritual wardrobe. Death is nothing more than

186

exchanging inferior clothing for superior clothing. That is something to look forward to, isn't it?

I wish I could tell you that every Christian faces death with great anticipation. But some believers, at the end of their lives, express regret about what they are missing on earth, even though they have faith about their future home in heaven. However, any sadness Christians feel over leaving this earth will be more than compensated for by the

> *Christians do not need to fear death as we make our way toward heaven.*

joy of heaven. I believe this is what Jesus had in mind when He promised, "Blessed are you who weep now, for you shall laugh" (Luke 6:21). Christians do not need to fear death as we make our way toward heaven.

How does the analogy of changing clothes for a new location help you understand what happens to us when we die and leave our bodies behind?

Lord, You have invited me to be with You for eternity. May I look forward with joyful anticipation to the day when You call me to leave this old body behind and put on my magnificent new spiritual clothes.

How to Prepare for Our Journey to Heaven

> Teach us to number our days, that we may present to You a heart of wisdom.
>
> —Psalm 90:12

How can you prepare for your journey to heaven? Make the most of your time on earth.

Before the flood of Noah's day, people on earth lived hundreds and hundreds of years. Genesis 5:27 tells us that Methuselah, the oldest man who ever lived, died at 969 years of age! Immediately after the flood, the average life span decreased dramatically. Gradually, through science, technology, and better nutrition, people's life spans started to increase. But did you know that now, for the first time in decades, the average life span has decreased once again?

Make the most of your time on earth.

While God has allotted a different number of years for every one of us in this life, in Psalm 90, Moses said there is an average life span for most people. He said, "As for the days of our life, they contain seventy years, or if due to strength, eighty years, yet their pride is but labor and sorrow; for soon it is gone and we fly away. . . . So teach us to number our days, that we may present to You a heart of wisdom" (90:10, 12).

I will never forget the first time I heard someone speak on these verses. I was a freshman at Baylor University sitting in an orientation chapel, pining for my girlfriend (now my wife), who was one hundred miles away at the University of Texas. It would be two weeks until I saw her, and Moses's observation about the brevity of time seemed profoundly untrue. Time moved like molasses back then! Yet the older I get, the more I understand what Moses was saying. As one wag put it, "Life is like a roll of toilet paper—the closer you get to the end, the more quickly it goes." You probably have discovered that, haven't you? That is what Moses was saying. "Teach us to number our days."

———

What does it mean to "number our days"?

How can you do this practically in your own life?

Why do you think numbering our days produces "a heart of wisdom"?

Lord, my time on earth is limited, and every passing moment brings me closer to the time when You will call me home. Give me Your perspective on my life span, and help me spend my time wisely in the days that remain.

Make the Most of Your Time on Earth

> Be careful how you walk, not as unwise men but as wise, making the most of your time, because the days are evil.
>
> —Ephesians 5:15–16

One way you can prepare for your journey to heaven is to make the most of your time on earth.

The apostle Paul said it this way in Ephesians 5:15–16: "Be careful how you walk, not as unwise men but as wise, making the most of your time, because the days are evil." In the Bible, the word *walk* is a metaphor for how you live your life. Paul was saying, "Be very careful how you live your life in light of how short your time is on earth."

Be very careful how you live your life in light of how short your time is on earth.

Here is a good exercise. Ask yourself, *What three things do I think God would have me to do before I die?* That is a good thing to sit down and think about for a while. Once you get those three things in your mind, then ask yourself, *As I go throughout the day, how much time do I actually devote to those major priorities in my life?* Most of us spend very little time doing the things we think are the most important. That is why Paul told us to make the most of our time.

The phrase translated "make the most" is a Greek word that literally means "buy up." Buy up your time. Time is a precious commodity. Somebody has said the difference between successful people and unsuccessful people is their tender, loving care for time. And as another person has said, "Time is the stuff life is made of. Life is like a dollar. You can spend it any way you want, but you can only spend it once." That is why Paul was saying, "You'd better buy it up. You'd better make the most of your time."

———————

What are some ways in which you tend to waste your time?
How could you make better use of those hours to fulfill your God-given priorities?

God, help me identify the three things You would have me do before I die. Then give me the wisdom and courage to make the most of the time You give me in this life to focus on doing what You have called me to do.

Live according to God's Plan for Your Life

Make the best use of your time, despite all the difficulties of these days.

—Ephesians 5:16 PHILLIPS

Henry David Thoreau was fearful he would come to the end of his life and realize he had not really lived his life. He feared that when the day of his death arrived, he would "discover that [he] had not lived." He wrote, "I did not wish to live what was not life. . . . I wanted to live deep and suck out all the marrow of life . . . to put to rout all that was not life, to cut a broad swath and shave close."[1] Thoreau's way of doing that was by going and living in the woods.

But the apostle Paul had a better idea for how to make the most of our time on earth. We can make the most of our time here by living in accordance with God's plan for our lives. Paul said, "[Make] the most of your time, because the days are evil" (Eph. 5:16). What did he mean by that? He simply meant that part of Satan's scheme for our lives is to lead us not only into doing sinful things but also into doing meaningless things, to fritter away our time not doing the things that really count.

We can make the most of our time here by living in accordance with God's plan for our lives.

Make no mistake: Satan will do whatever it takes to prevent you from living a purposeful and God-honoring life. Satan will entice you to squander your time (and therefore your life) on worthless pursuits rather than your God-given priorities in life.

I like the way J. B. Phillips paraphrased Ephesians 5:15–17:

Live life, then, with a due sense of responsibility, not as men who do not know the meaning and purpose of life but as those who do. Make the best use of your time, despite all the difficulties of these days. Don't be vague but firmly grasp what you know to be the will of God. (PHILLIPS)

Make the most of your time.

———

Are you squandering your time on worthless pursuits?

How can you maximize your time today to focus on your God-given priorities?

Lord, help me make the most of my time in this life by focusing on Your kingdom and the hope of my heavenly home.

Minimize Your Predeparture Regrets

> Forgetting what lies behind and reaching forward
> to what lies ahead, I press on toward the goal for
> the prize of the upward call of God in Christ Jesus.
> —Philippians 3:13–14

To prepare for your journey to heaven, you must minimize your predeparture regrets.

Have you ever been at the departure gate getting ready to get on a plane, and you remember something you should have done? You suddenly realize, *I should have stopped the newspaper. I should have stopped the mail. I should have packed a warmer coat or an extra pair of socks.* You know what I am talking about. You wish you had done something, but it is too late. Now, those kinds of regrets are real, but they have no lasting consequences. They are also trivial compared to the deep regrets many people feel as they prepare to leave this world for the next one. If you come to the end of your life ready to enter into heaven with regrets, then that is a whole different story.

Nothing will steal your joy faster or devour your days more completely than regrets.

As a pastor, I have had the experience many times of sitting with Christians who were about to die and listening to them lament their regrets in life: relationships they wish they had maximized, relationships they wished they had not broken, opportunities they should have taken advantage of. Nothing will steal your joy faster or devour your days more completely than regrets.

I am reminded of the words of poet John Greenleaf Whittier, who wrote, "For all sad words of tongue or pen, the saddest are these: 'It might have been.'"[1] But God wants us to live in such a way that when He calls us to heaven, we are not filled with predeparture regrets.

What are some common regrets that people experience?

How does regret steal our joy?

Lord, give me the courage to seize opportunities, mend relationships, and build a life that is pleasing to You. Help me live in such a way that I will come to the end of my life ready to enter into heaven with no regrets.

Live without Regrets

A joyful heart makes a cheerful face, but when the
heart is sad, the spirit is broken.
—Proverbs 15:13

Regrets are like a cancer. They eat at the very core of our being,
and that is certainly no way to spend our final days here on
earth.

When I think about some of the most common regrets of
those who are dying, I think about my own dad. My father
was a successful man by any standard.
He was a faithful follower of Christ. He
led my mom to faith in Christ, and he
led his children to become Christians
as well. My father held an important
position in the airline industry, en-
joyed an upper-middle-class income, traveled the world, was
respected by colleagues and friends, and was deeply loved by
his family.

> *Regrets are like a
> cancer. They eat at the
> very core of our being.*

Yet when my father was sixty-six years of age, the doc-
tors informed him that he had pancreatic cancer and had
only four months to live. During those months preceding his
death, I spent a lot of time with my father, sitting with him
and listening to him lament the "what ifs" and "if onlys" of
his life. He regretted the trips he wished he had taken, career
opportunities he didn't maximize, words he should not have
spoken, and relationships he didn't fully appreciate. He even

regretted not wearing the new suits he had purchased for fear of wearing them out.

My dad's final months on this earth were not altogether happy ones. Through his experience, I learned that regrets have the power to extinguish the joy of an otherwise happy life. I also learned that in the end, someone else is either going to sell or give away your clothes—just as we did with my dad's suits—so you might as well wear them today.

———

What do you think you will regret on your deathbed?

What step can you take today to avoid experiencing that regret when death comes?

Lord, when the appointed day of my death comes, I don't want to lament the "what ifs" and "if onlys" of my life. Show me how to live fully today so that I can leave this earth without regrets, leaving behind a legacy of faithfulness and joy.

Focus on What God Wants You to Do

> Don't be vague but firmly grasp what you know to
> be the will of God.
>
> —Ephesians 5:17 PHILLIPS

As you prepare for your journey to heaven, one of the best resolutions you can make is to get rid of any unnecessary regrets. How can you make sure that you do not end your life with a long list of regrets? One way to do this is to evaluate your life honestly.

Here is an exercise you can do that would honor God. Take a sheet of paper and divide it into five columns, representing the five major areas of your life: your relationship with God, your relationship with family, your relationship with friends, your career, and your finances. Then ask God to help you identify three things you would like to accomplish in each of these areas before you go to heaven. Ask yourself, *What are the three things God would like me to concentrate on during the remaining years I have on earth?* Under each column, write three goals you would like to achieve in each of these life areas before you die.

I encourage you to write your goals in the form of resolutions for each of these major life areas. For example, when it comes to your relationship with God: "Resolved: I will glorify God so that He will say, 'Well done, good and faithful servant.'" Or regarding your family: "Resolved: I will appreciate, enjoy, and value the mate God gave me." Or regarding your children: "Resolved: I will endeavor to point my children to Christ, to earn their respect, and to celebrate their uniqueness." Or with your friends: "Resolved: I will treasure my friendships by praying for and spending time with those people who enrich my life." When it comes to your career: "Resolved:

Focus on those things you believe God would have you to do regardless of how long He leaves you here on earth.

I will choose a life work that utilizes my giftedness and my passions." When it comes to your finances: "Resolved: I will make sure that my finances are in order and my family is provided for when I die."

One of the best resolutions you can make right now is to focus on those things you believe God would have you to do regardless of how long He leaves you here on earth.

What goals did you write down for each major area of your life? What specific steps will you take to accomplish those goals?

God, give me Your wisdom and perspective as I honestly evaluate my life. Show me how to focus on the things You want me to do during my remaining years on earth.

Deal with Past Mistakes

> I have fought the good fight, I have finished the
> course, I have kept the faith.
>
> —2 Timothy 4:7

How can you make sure that you do not end your life with a long list of regrets? Part of dealing with regrets is dealing with your past mistakes.

When the apostle Paul was facing death, he knew he had made terrible errors. He had persecuted Christians. He did not come to the end of his life without mistakes, but he was without any regrets. In 2 Timothy 4:7, as Paul prepared for his execution, he said, "I have fought the good fight, I have finished the course, I have kept the faith."

As you evaluate your life, maybe you feel badly about mistakes you've made, opportunities you've squandered, or people you've hurt. It is impossible to erase the past. Life has no rewind button. But with God's help, you can allow your errors to be stepping-stones. You can make some changes in your life right now that will reshape both your tomorrow and your eternity. If you don't believe that, consider the story of one Swedish philanthropist.

You can make some changes in your life right now that will reshape both your tomorrow and your eternity.

Alfred Nobel was a chemist who made his fortune by inventing dynamite. Though intended for commercial construction, dynamite was quickly adapted by governments into an instrument of war. When his brother Ludvig died in 1888, French newspapers confused Ludvig for Alfred and mistakenly reported, "The merchant of death is dead." When Alfred Nobel read his obituary and realized he would be remembered only for enabling the killing of millions of people, he decided to dedicate the rest of his life to scientific, artistic, and peaceful endeavors that celebrated humanity. He set aside a sizable sum of his vast wealth and established the Nobel prizes we're familiar with today.

Few of us will achieve the fame and fortune of Alfred Nobel, but all of us can deal with our past mistakes by redirecting our time, our money, and our energy to things that will allow us to die without regrets.

––––––––––

If you died today, what would your obituary say?
What changes can you make in your life to change the way you will be remembered?

God, You know all the mistakes I've made, people I've hurt, and opportunities I've squandered. I confess those sins to You and accept Your forgiveness for them. Help me turn those mistakes into stepping-stones that lead me into the glorious future You have planned for me.

Take Care of the Practical Matters before You Depart

> Set your house in order, for you shall die and not live.
>
> —2 Kings 20:1

You can prepare for your journey to heaven by taking care of the practical matters while you're still able. Before you depart this world, make sure that those you care about most are adequately provided for.

In the Old Testament, the prophet Isaiah went to King Hezekiah with a sobering message. He told the king, "Set your house in order, for you shall die and not live" (2 Kings 20:1). That is good advice for all of us. Set your house in order, because someday you are going to die.

Set your house in order, because someday you are going to die.

When I think about making preparations for loved ones before death comes, I think about a friend of mine who attended a seminar about making financial preparations in the event of a spouse's death. When my friend returned from the conference, he had a frank discussion with his wife about what she should do if he preceded her in death. "Honey," he said, "I think you should plan to stay in the house since the mortgage is almost paid." She agreed. "And if you choose to remarry, that is fine with me. In fact, I would have no problem with your new husband and you occupying our bedroom." Again, no disagreement from his wife. "Also, I would want him to feel free to use my golf clubs if he was as passionate about the game as I am," he added. "Oh, no! That would never work!" my friend's wife said. "Why not?" her husband wondered. She said, "Because you're right-handed, and he's left-handed!"

That is a funny story, but what is not is a scenario I've seen played out far too many times: a spouse dies without discussing financial affairs, the location of his or her will or life insurance policies (if either exist), security passwords, funeral desires, or other vital information with the surviving spouse or children. The result is that the family is in the dark about these critical issues, leading them to waste energy and time that should be directed to grieving and recovery.

The fact is, death is inevitable. Someday, you are going to die and leave your loved ones behind. Have you made adequate preparation for your death? Do that for your family. You won't regret it, and neither will they.

––––––––

What preparations have you made for your family in the event of your death?
Make it a priority to take care of those practical matters before it's too late.

Lord, I admit that I don't like thinking about the inevitable day of my death. Give me the courage to set my house in order by having important conversations and taking care of the practical matters that demonstrate my care for the loved ones I leave behind.

Are You Ready for Your Journey to Heaven?

> [He] died in a ripe old age, an old man and satisfied with life; and he was gathered to his people.
> —Genesis 25:8

The early deaths of both of my parents had a profound effect on my life. Both were strong believers who taught me not only how to live as a Christian but also how to die as a Christian. Their premature deaths (at least from my perspective) steeled my resolve to live without regrets and to die without regrets.

If I were to compose my own epitaph for my headstone, I could not come up with anything better than the one engraved for Abraham: "[He] died in a ripe old age, an old man and satisfied with life; and he was gathered to his people" (Gen. 25:8). Abraham came to the end of his life without a long list of "if onlys" or "what ifs." He was content with his past, knowing his mistakes had been forgiven by God. He was satisfied with his present, knowing he had passed along his faith in God to his children and grandchildren. And he was at peace with his future, having prepared for his journey to be

If you are a Christian, you need not fear the journey, especially when you consider the destination.

gathered to his people and with his God because of his faith in God's provision for his sin. Abraham died satisfied with life.

Are you ready for your journey to heaven? If you are a Christian, you need not fear the journey, especially when you consider the destination. It is a place more magnificent than you could ever imagine. It is a place where every heartache will be erased and every dream will be fulfilled. It is more glorious than mere words can begin to describe. It is a place reserved for those who have trusted in Christ as their Savior.

It is a place called heaven.

———————

Are you ready for your journey to heaven?
Whom can you tell today about the hope of heaven?

God, help me live in such a way that I, too, will come to the end of my life content with my past, satisfied with my present, and at peace with my future. Thank You for preparing a magnificent, glorious home for me in that place called heaven.

Acknowledgments

No book is a solo effort. I'm deeply indebted to the following people who were tremendously helpful in creating and communicating this encouraging message about *A Place Called Heaven*:

Brian Vos, Mark Rice, Brianna DeWitt, Lindsey Spoolstra, and the entire team at Baker Publishing Group, who caught the vision for this book immediately.

Jennifer Stair, who did a masterful job of adapting my original book, *A Place Called Heaven*, into a daily devotional that will keep our minds centered "on the things above."

Derrick Jeter, our creative director at Pathway to Victory, who was an invaluable help to me in the development of my original book, *A Place Called Heaven.*

Sealy Yates, my literary agent and friend for more than twenty years, who always provides sound advice and "outside the lines" creativity.

Carrilyn Baker, my faithful associate for nearly two decades, who helped keep track of the numerous drafts of this book while juggling a multitude of other tasks at the same time—and always with excellence.

Ben Lovvorn, Nate Curtis, Patrick Heatherington, Ben Bugg, and the entire Pathway to Victory team, who share the message of this book with millions of people throughout the world.

Amy Jeffress, my junior high girlfriend and wife of more than forty years, who makes everything I am able to do possible.

Notes

Day 2 Homesick for Heaven

1. Philip Yancey, *Disappointment with God: Three Questions No One Asks Aloud* (Grand Rapids: Zondervan, 1988), 276.

Day 4 Learning to Number Our Days

1. Joni Eareckson Tada, *Heaven: Your Real Home* (Grand Rapids: Zondervan, 1995), 15.

Day 5 Perspectives from the Past

1. C. S. Lewis, *Mere Christianity* (San Francisco: HarperSanFrancisco, 2001), 134.

Day 20 Have Some People Already Visited Heaven?

1. "Dwight L. Moody Is Dead," *New York Times*, December 23, 1899, accessed January 13, 2020, http://www.nytimes.com/1899/12/23/archives/dwight-l-moody-is-dead-succumbs-at-his-east-northfield-mass-home-to.html.

2. International Association for Near-Death Studies, "Near-Death Experiences: Key Facts," accessed January 13, 2020, http://iands.org/images/stories/pdf_downloads/Key%20Facts%20Handout-brochure-small.pdf.

Day 26 There Is One Fate for All

1. Randy Alcorn, *Heaven* (Carol Stream, IL: Tyndale, 2004), xix.

Day 27 Why Do People Have to Die?

1. Jack Nicholson, as quoted in Ron Rhodes, *The Wonder of Heaven: A Biblical Tour of Our Eternal Home* (Eugene, OR: Harvest House, 2009), 26–27.

Day 36 Heaven Is Not Boring

1. G. K. Chesterton, *Orthodoxy* (Wheaton, IL: Harold Shaw Publishers, 1994), 61.

Day 56 Citizens of Heaven Are Aware of the Captives in Hell

1. Warren Wiersbe, *The Wiersbe Bible Commentary: New Testament* (Colorado Springs: David C. Cook, 2007), 1079.

Day 66 Our Resurrection Bodies Will Be Perfect and Personal

1. Joni Eareckson Tada, *Heaven: Your Real Home* (Grand Rapids: Zondervan, 1995), 76.

Day 84 Our Spiritual Passport to Heaven

1. Elliot Blair Smith, "Warren Buffett Signs Over $30.7 Billion to the Bill and Melinda Gates Foundation," *USA Today*, June 26, 2006.

Day 94 Live according to God's Plan for Your Life

1. Henry David Thoreau, *Walden, or Life in the Woods* (New York: Everyman's Library, 1910), 80–81.

Day 95 Minimize Your Pre-departure Regrets

1. John Greenleaf Whittier, "Maud Muller," in *The Poems of John Greenleaf Whittier* (Boston: James R. Osgood and Co., 1878), 206.

About the Author

Dr. Robert Jeffress is senior pastor of the fourteen-thousand-member First Baptist Church, Dallas, Texas, and a Fox News contributor. He is also an adjunct professor at Dallas Theological Seminary. Dr. Jeffress has made more than two thousand guest appearances on various radio and television programs and regularly appears on major mainstream media outlets such as Fox News channel's *Fox and Friends*, *The O'Reilly Factor*, *Hannity*, *Lou Dobbs Tonight*, *Varney and Co.*, and *Judge Jeanine*; ABC's *Good Morning America*; and HBO's *Real Time with Bill Maher*. Dr. Jeffress hosts a daily radio program, *Pathway to Victory*, that is heard nationwide on over one thousand stations in major markets such as Dallas–Fort Worth, New York City, Chicago, Los Angeles, Houston, Washington, DC, San Francisco, Philadelphia, and Seattle. His daily television program, *Pathway to Victory*, can be seen Monday through Friday on the Trinity Broadcasting Network (TBN), every Sunday on TBN, and daily on the Hillsong Channel. *Pathway to Victory* is the second-highest rated ministry program on TBN's Sunday schedule. Dr. Jeffress's television broadcast reaches 195 countries and is on 11,295 cable and satellite systems throughout the world.

Dr. Jeffress is the author of twenty-six books, including *Not All Roads Lead to Heaven*, *A Place Called Heaven*, *Choosing the Extraordinary Life*, *Courageous*, and *Praying for America*. Dr. Jeffress recently led his congregation in the completion of a $135 million re-creation of its downtown campus. The project is the largest in modern church history and serves as a "spiritual oasis" covering six blocks of downtown Dallas.

Dr. Jeffress has a DMin from Southwestern Baptist Theological Seminary, a ThM from Dallas Theological Seminary, and a BS from Baylor University. In May 2010, he was awarded a Doctor of Divinity degree from Dallas Baptist University, and in June 2011, he received the Distinguished Alumnus of the Year award from Southwestern Baptist Theological Seminary.

Dr. Jeffress and his wife, Amy, have two daughters and three grandchildren.

Your Road Map to a Life of
ETERNAL IMPACT

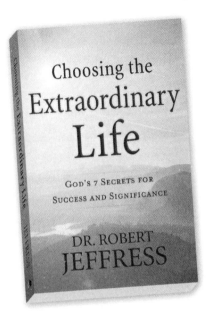

In this inspiring and motivating book, Dr. Jeffress reveals seven secrets from Elijah that result in a life marked by significance, satisfaction, and success, including

- · discovering your unique purpose in life
- · waiting on God's timing
- · learning how to handle bad days
- · and more

For anyone who wonders if there's more to life—God's Word reveals seven secrets for experiencing a truly extraordinary life.

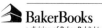

Teach Your Little Ones about
HEAVEN

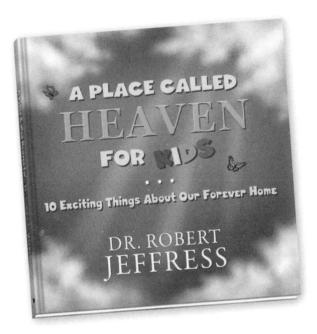

Colorfully illustrated and using simple concepts and language that children ages 4–7 can understand, this book gives children peace of mind about their lost loved one as well as a comforting, biblical picture of their forever home. For parents, grandparents, and caregivers, it offers a positive, constructive way to grieve, hope, and grow—together.

A PLACE CALLED
HEAVEN

The Complete Teaching Series on
DVD Video & MP3-format Audio Disc

» Includes all twelve messages from the teaching series by
Dr. Jeffress in their original, unedited form

» The full-color ministry resource, "What Seven World
Religions Teach About Heaven", is also available to order
with the set

NOT ALL ROADS LEAD TO HEAVEN

The Complete Teaching Series on DVD Video & MP3-format Audio Disc

Resources available include...

» *Not All Roads Lead to Heaven*, plus "Christianity, Cults, & Religions"— a side-by-side comparison chart of sixteen groups

» The complete series on DVD/MP3-format audio disc

» A comprehensive ten-week Bible study guidebook, complete with answers to study questions and expanded responses to key points

COURAGEOUS
LEADER KIT

Leader kit resources include...

» One copy of the book *Courageous*

» A set of ten *Courageous* encouragement cards

» The complete series on DVD/MP3-format audio disc

» A personal and group study guide, complete with answers to study questions and expanded responses to key points

» *Courageous* leader kit storage box